THE
PASSION
TRANSLATION

THE PASSIONATE LIFE BIBLE STUDY SERIES

12-LESSON STUDY GUIDE

THE BOOK OF
GENESIS

PART ONE
Chapters 1-11

firstfruits

BroadStreet
PUBLISHING

BroadStreet Publishing® Group, LLC
Savage, Minnesota, USA
BroadStreetPublishing.com

TPT: The Book of Genesis – Part 1: 12-Lesson Bible Study Guide
Copyright © 2022 BroadStreet Publishing Group

978-1-4245-6093-6 (softcover)
978-1-4245-6094-3 (e-book)

Unless otherwise noted, Scripture quotations are from The Passion Translation®, copyright © 2017, 2018, 2020 by Passion & Fire Ministries, Inc. Used by permission. All rights reserved. Scripture quotations marked NASB are taken from the New American Standard Bible® (NASB), copyright © 1960, 1962, 1963, 1968, 1971, 1972, 1973, 1975, 1977, 1995, 2020 by The Lockman Foundation. Used by permission. www.Lockman.org. Scripture quotations marked NIV are taken from The Holy Bible, New International Version® NIV®. Copyright © 1973, 1978, 1984, 2011 by Biblica, Inc.™ Used by permission. All rights reserved worldwide. Scripture quotations marked NLT are taken from the Holy Bible, New Living Translation, copyright © 1996, 2004, 2015 by Tyndale House Foundation. Used by permission of Tyndale House Publishers, a Division of Tyndale House Ministries, Carol Stream, Illinois 60188. All rights reserved.

Stock or custom editions of BroadStreet Publishing titles may be purchased in bulk for educational, business, ministry, fundraising, or sales promotional use. For information, please email orders@broadstreetpublishing.com.

General editor: Brian Simmons
Managing editor: William D. Watkins
Writer: William D. Watkins

Design and typesetting | garborgdesign.com

Printed in the United States of America

22 23 24 25 26 5 4 3 2 1

Contents

From God's Heart to Yours

"God is love," says the apostle John, and "Everyone who loves is fathered by God and experiences an intimate knowledge of him" (1 John 4:7). The life of a Christ-follower is, at its core, a life of love—God's love of us, our love of him, and our love of others and ourselves because of God's love for us.

And this divine love is reliable, trustworthy, unconditional, other-centered, majestic, forgiving, redemptive, patient, kind, and more precious than anything else we can ever receive or give. It characterizes each person of the Trinity—Father, Son, and Holy Spirit—and so is as unlimited as they are. They love one another with this eternal love, and they reach beyond themselves to us, created in their image with this love.

How do we know such incredible truths? Through the primary source of all else we know about the one God—his Word, the Bible. Of course, God reveals who he is through other sources as well, such as the natural world, miracles, our inner life, our relationships (especially with him), those who minister on his behalf, and those who proclaim him to us and others. But the fullest and most comprehensive revelation we have of God and from him is what he has given us in the thirty-nine books of the Hebrew Scriptures (the Old Testament) and the twenty-seven books of the Christian Scriptures (the New Testament). Together, these sixty-six books present a compelling and telling portrait of God and his dealings with us.

It is these Scriptures that *The Passionate Life Bible Study Series* is all about. Through these study guides, we—the editors and writers of this series—seek to provide you with a unique and welcoming opportunity to delve more deeply into God's precious Word, encountering there his loving heart for you and all the others he loves. God wants you to know him more deeply, to love him more devoutly, and to share his heart with others more frequently and freely. To accomplish this, we have based this study guide series on The Passion Translation of the Bible, which strives to "unlock the passion of [God's] heart." It is "a heart-level translation, from the passion of God's heart to the passion of your heart," created to "kindle in you a burning desire for him and his heart, while impacting the church for years to come."[1]

In each study guide, you will find an introduction to the Bible book it covers. There you will gain information about that Bible book's authorship, date of composition, first recipients, setting, purpose, central message, and key themes. Each lesson following the introduction will take a portion of that Bible book and walk you through it so you will learn its content better while experiencing and applying God's heart for your own life and encountering ways you can share his heart with others. Along the way, you will come across a number of features we have created that provide opportunities for more life application and growth in biblical understanding:

 ## Experience God's Heart

This feature focuses questions on personal application. It will help you live out God's Word, to bring the Bible into your world in fresh, exciting, and relevant ways.

 ## Share God's Heart

This feature will help you grow in your ability to share with other people what you learn and apply in a given lesson. It provides guidance on how the lesson relates to growing closer to others, to enriching your fellowship with others. It also points the way to enabling you to better listen to the stories of others so you can bridge the biblical story with their stories.

The Backstory

This feature provides ancient historical and cultural background that illuminates Bible passages and teachings. It deals with then-pertinent religious groups, communities, leaders, disputes, business trades, travel routes, customs, nations, political factions, ancient measurements and currency...in short, anything historical or cultural that will help you better understand what Scripture says and means. You may also find maps and charts that will help you reimagine these groups, places, and activities. Finally, in this feature you will find references to additional Bible texts that will further illuminate the Scripture you are studying.

 ## Word Wealth

This feature provides definitions and other illuminating information about key terms, names, and concepts, and how different ancient languages have influenced the biblical text. It also provides insight into the different literary forms in the Bible, such as prophecy, poetry, narrative history, parables, and letters, and how knowing the form of a text can help you better interpret and apply it. Finally, this feature highlights the most significant passages in a Bible book. You may be encouraged to memorize these verses or keep them before you in some way so you can actively hide God's Word in your heart.

 ## Digging Deeper

This feature explains the theological significance of a text or the controversial issues that arise and mentions resources you can use to help you arrive at your own conclusions. Another way to dig deeper into the Word is by looking into the life of a biblical character or another person from church history, showing how that man or woman incarnated a biblical truth or passage. For instance, Jonathan Edwards was well known for his missions work among native American Indians and for his intellectual prowess in articulating the Christian faith; Florence Nightingale for the reforms she brought about in healthcare; Irenaeus for his fight against heresy; Billy Graham for his work in evangelism; Moses for the strength God gave him to lead the Hebrews and receive and communicate the law; Deborah for her work as a judge in Israel. This feature introduces to you figures from the past who model what it looks like to experience God's heart and share his heart with others.

The Extra Mile

While The Passion Translation's notes are extensive, sometimes students of Scripture like to explore more on their own. In this feature, we provide you with opportunities to glean more information from a Bible dictionary, a Bible encyclopedia, a reliable Bible online tool, another ancient text, and the like. Here you will learn how you can go the extra mile on a Bible lesson. And not just in study either. Reflection, prayer, discussion, and applying a passage in new ways provide even more opportunities to go the extra mile. Here you will find questions to answer and applications to make that will require more time and energy from you—if and when you have them to give.

As you can see above, each of these features has a corresponding icon so you can quickly and easily identify them.

You will find other helps and guidance through the lessons of these study guides, including thoughtful questions, application suggestions, and spaces for you to record your own reflections, answers, and action steps. Of course, you can also write in your own journal, notebook, computer, or other resource, but we have provided you with space for your convenience.

Also, each lesson will direct you into the introductory material and numerous notes provided in The Passion Translation. There each Bible book contains a number of aids supplied to help you better grasp God's words and his incredible love, power, knowledge, plans, and so much more. We want you to get the most out of your Bible study, especially using it to draw you closer to the One who loves you most.

Finally, at the end of each lesson you'll find a section called "Talking It Out." This contains questions and exercises for application that you can share, answer, and apply with your spouse, a friend, a coworker, a Bible study group, or any other individuals or groups who would like to walk with you through this material. As Christians, we gather together to serve, study, worship, sing, evangelize, and a host of other activities. We grow together, not just on our own. This section will give you ample opportunities to engage others with the content of each lesson so you can work it out in community.

We offer all of this to support you in becoming an even more faithful and loving disciple of Jesus Christ. A disciple in the ancient world was a student of her teacher, a follower of his master. Students study and followers follow. Jesus' disciples are to sit at his feet and listen and learn and then do what he tells them and shows them to do. We have created The Passionate Life Bible Study Series to help you do what a disciple of Jesus is called to do.

So go.

Read God's words.

Hear what he has to say in them and through them.

Meditate on them.

Hide them in your heart.

Display their truths in your life.

Share their truths with others.

Let them ignite Jesus' passion and light in all you say and do.

Use them to help you fulfill what Jesus called his disciples to do: "'Now go in my authority and make disciples of all nations, baptizing them in the name of the Father, the Son, and the Holy Spirit. And teach them to faithfully follow all that I have commanded you. And never forget that I am with you every day, even to the completion of this age'" (Matthew 28:19–20).

And through all of this, let Jesus' love nourish your heart and allow that love to overflow into your relationships with others (John 15:9–13). For it was for love that Jesus came, served, died, rose from the dead, and ascended into heaven. This love he gives us. And this love he wants us to pass along to others.

Why I Love the Book of Genesis

I love Genesis because it keeps me on the edge of my seat. Even reading the genealogies excites me. Every Bible reader needs to begin at the beginning, and what a beginning it is! Genesis starts off with a bang—a big bang! It will hold your attention from the very start as the cosmic silence is broken by the thunderous voice of God Almighty creating a universe.

Genesis also gives away God's secrets. One way to discover the true value of something is to imagine not having it. Can you imagine if we did not have a book called Genesis? We would have no clue about:

- creation's artistry
- the delight of God's heart in forming human beings
- his eternal plan to express covenant love to men and women
- the blessing of heaven
- his choosing special servants to change the world

I love Genesis as well because it reveals the God of Glory, our kind Creator, who searches us out when we have erred and wandered from his presence. The transcendent God is unveiled through his creation and through his kindness to all. He is seen as holy, loving, and merciful as we turn the pages of this epic blockbuster. Genesis shows us the character and power of God. You can see grace and holiness holding hands and walking together through the story line of this masterpiece. We see who God is, what he can do, and how he relates to the people he made. Understanding who he has revealed himself to be helps us gain a better understanding of who we are and how we are to live in this world.

I love Genesis because of all the promises God has made and kept. He promised a coming "seed" who would redeem humanity and break the curse from our planet. He promised to protect and preserve Noah and his family even in a time of judgment. He promised to bless Abraham and his sons and grandsons. He promised Joseph that his brothers would one day bow down to him. God keeps every promise he makes, and he will keep every promise he has given to you and me. Genesis convinces me that God is faithful.

And I love Genesis because I see my life in the journey of those who followed the voice of God. Abraham teaches me about faith. Isaac shows me the path of sonship and inheritance. Jacob persuades me that God will transform everything in me that doesn't reflect Christ. And Joseph maps out for me the path that every true prince or princess who is destined to reign must walk—a path filled with both testing and triumph.

Because Genesis is so foundational to the rest of history, we've decided to cover it in two study guides. This one treats the first eleven chapters of Genesis, from creation to the confusion of human languages during the construction of the tower of Babel. The second study guide treats the rest of Genesis, from God's choice of Abraham to the last days of Jacob and Joseph—the era of the Patriarchs. I hope you will take the next several weeks to pour through the pages of this first part of the Genesis Bible study guides. Take notes, underline what speaks to you, and answer the questions we pose. Genesis will lead you into a deeper understanding of God and the way he works in your life. Let him speak to you and enflame you with a passion to follow God with faith and courage. I know you are going to love Genesis too!

Brian Simmons
General Editor

Genesis: The Book of Origins

Every story has a starting place, every life a beginning, every plot an opening narrative. History is no exception. All the major characters, events, inventions, lessons learned and lost...have an origin. The lone exception is God, who eternally lives above the changing universe and all it contains. In fact, he is the One who brought this universe into existence and inhabited it with living creatures. How do we know this? Genesis.

Genesis is the book of origins, given to us by God to reveal his work in creation and his involvement in history, especially in human history. Genesis gives us God's perspective on such events as:

- the beginning of the universe
- the beginning of the earth
- the beginning of order in creation
- the beginning of life in creation
- the beginning of God's self-revelation
- the beginning of humanity
- the beginning of humanity's fellowship with God
- the beginning of marriage
- the beginning of God's blessing upon humanity
- the beginning of Satan's war against God on earth

- the beginning of human sin, death, and nature's corruption
- the beginning of God's plan to defeat evil and redeem the sin-ridden created order
- the beginning of marital discord
- the beginning of families and fractures
- the beginning of faith and doubt
- the beginning of human culture and civilization
- the beginning of the division of human language
- the beginning of God's covenants with human beings
- the beginning of God's love poured through and on creation, especially on humanity

All the beginnings that are the most important for us to know are provided in the inspired historical record of Genesis.

- *If you were writing a history of your life, what are two or three beginnings you would include that have had the most impact on you? Why does each one matter so much?*

The Book's Title

The Hebrew title of the book comes from the opening Hebrew phrase, *bereshith*, usually translated "in the beginning" or "when." The English title, "Genesis," comes from the Greek word *geneseos*, which appears in the Septuagint, the first Greek translation of the Old Testament. The Septuagint was commissioned during the middle of the third century BCE, and it was during this time that the Pentateuch (Genesis through Deuteronomy) was completely translated from Hebrew into Greek.[2] The Greek word *geneseos* can be translated a number of ways, including "origin," "birth," "history of origin," "genealogy," or "account," depending on the context in which the word appears (e.g., Genesis 2:4, "account").[3]

Whether we go with the Hebrew or Greek title, the content of Genesis focuses on firsts or beginnings and then starts to trace their development in history. As you will discover, the historical accounts key in on the most important happenings—what and who matters the most in the revelation of God's significant undertakings in earthly history. These are the people and events he wants us to know about in the stories of creation, paradise, the fall and its consequences, and his remedy for human rebellion.

- *Why do you think books of history focus on key people, events, and ideas and not on everything that happened during the time period covered?*

- *What makes the origin of something so important?*

- *Look at the list of beginnings provided at the start of this lesson. Take just a few of them and write below why you think it's important that we know about each one, especially given that God has chosen to reveal them to us.*

Authorship

Genesis is the first book of the Torah, also referred to as the law or the Pentateuch. The other books of the Torah are Exodus, Leviticus, Numbers, and Deuteronomy. Most likely the earliest division of the Hebrew Scriptures was twofold: the Torah and the Prophets (the latter including the rest of the Old Testament books). Eventually, however, the Jews divided the Hebrew Scriptures into three major sections: the Torah, the Prophets, and the Writings.[4]

In Scripture, Moses and the Torah (or law) are often linked, which is why there's a long-standing tradition that ascribes Moses as the author of Genesis.

- *Look up the following passages. Write down what you find about Moses and the law.*

Deuteronomy 31:9–13

Joshua 1:7–8

1 Kings 2:1–3

Malachi 4:4

Luke 24:44

John 1:17

Acts 13:38–39

Acts 26:22–23

• *What do some of the passages teach about who revealed the law to Moses? Is the law's source Moses or God?*

• *What are people expected to do in light of the Mosaic law?*

THE BACKSTORY

Moses was certainly suited for the task of writing Genesis and the rest of the Torah. Bible scholar Bruce K. Waltke states, "Moses' superb training, exceptional spiritual gifts and divine call uniquely qualified him to compose the essential content and shape of Genesis and of the Pentateuch." Among the many reasons Waltke and other scholars cite is the education Moses would have received "in Pharaoh's court as the son of Pharaoh's daughter (Ex. 2:1–10)."[5] Acts tells us that "Moses was fully trained in the royal courts [of Egypt] and educated in the highest wisdom Egypt had to offer" (Acts 7:22). That would have included ready access to ancient Near Eastern myths that offered different and conflicting creation and flood stories and accounts of kings, gods, and religious practices that Genesis 1–11 counters.

Moses, in his training to become an Egyptian leader, would have also learned the law codes of his native land as well as the ones that likely influenced them. One of these, the Code of Hammurabi (ca. 1700 BCE), shows some resemblances to the Book of the Covenant (Exodus 20:22–23:19), and "Deuteronomy has formal similarities with Hittite suzerainty treaties (1400–1250) at the time of Moses."[6]

Also, Waltke points out that:

> As the greatest of Israel's prophets, Moses
> would also have had the ability to draw upon
> God's omniscience and omnipresence in
> the retelling of Israel's historical traditions
> (cf. Num. 11:25; Deut. 34:10–11). With
> his extraordinary gift, confirmed by his
> spectacular signs and wonders, he was
> eminently qualified to usher his audience into
> the heavenly court at the time God created
> the cosmos (Gen. 1) and to reveal what the
> Almighty and other humans thought, felt, and
> intended (6:6, 8; 13:13; 25:34b).[7]

Finally, the author of Genesis and the rest of the Torah shows a great deal of knowledge about Egypt and Sinai, knowledge best acquired by someone like Moses who lived and traveled in those areas. Old Testament scholar Gleason L. Archer Jr. recounts some of this evidence, which includes:

- "Eyewitness details...in the account of the Exodus which suggest an actual participant in the events...For example, in Ex. 15:27 the narrator recalls the exact number of fountains (twelve) and of palm trees (seventy) at Elim"—a place in Sinai.

- "The author of Genesis and Exodus...is familiar with Egyptian names," such as the native name for Heliopolis and Pithom and "the special title of honor bestowed on Joseph by Pharaoh" in Genesis 41:45.

- The ancient author "also uses a greater percentage of Egyptian words than elsewhere in the Old Testament."

- The Genesis writer also uses "a large number of idioms and turns of speech that are characteristically Egyptian in origin, even though translated into Hebrew."

- "The titles of the [Egyptian] court officials, the polite language used in the interviews with Pharaoh, and the like are all...true to Egyptian usage."

- "The seasons and the weather referred to in the [Torah] narrative are Egyptian, not Palestinian."

- "The flora and fauna referred to are Egyptian or Sinaitic, never distinctively Palestinian."

- "The lists of clean and unclean birds and animals contained in Lev. 11 and Deut. 14 include some which are peculiar to Sinai...but none of which are peculiar to Canaan."

- "Both Egypt and Sinai are very familiar to the author from the standpoint of geography. The narrative of the Exodus route is filled with authentic local references that have been verified by modern archaeology."[8]

In short, Moses had the education, the knowledge, the skills, the experience, and so much more to accomplish all that God had for him to do, including writing Genesis and the rest of the Torah while leading God's people out of Egypt and up to the border of Canaan.

- *Do you know what God has prepared you to do? It can be great or small, public or private, within a church ministry or outside of it. But it will use your knowledge, experience, skills, education, and giftedness to accomplish what the Lord wants you to do—and it can be more than one thing! If you're not sure yet, that's all right. Ask God to guide you and, in his time, to reveal to you what he has for you to do. If you already know what God has for you, articulate it here and ask him to grant you anything else you need to do his will his way.*

Date of Writing

Genesis and the rest of the Torah were likely written after God's delivery of the Hebrews from slavery in Egypt but before Joshua led the people into Canaan, the promised land. This would place the Torah's composition during the Hebrews' forty years of wanderings in the Sinai wilderness. Gleason Archer writes: "[Moses] certainly had plenty of time and leisure during the slow, tiresome forty years of wandering in the Sinai desert to compose a book several times the size of the Torah."⁹

So when was this forty-year period? Here's how scholars arrive at this. First Kings 6:1 puts the start of Solomon's construction of the temple in Jerusalem during the fourth year of his reign and 480 years "after the Israelites came out of Egypt" (NIV). Solomon's fourth year was 966 BCE, and 480 years before that would put the exodus event at 1446. Soon after that, due to God's judgment on them, the Hebrews spent about forty years in Sinai before God commissioned Joshua to lead his people into Canaan (Exodus 16:35; Numbers 14:22–35; Deuteronomy 31:23; 34:9; Joshua 1:1–9). So between 1446 and about 1406, Moses wrote the Torah.¹⁰

His work on the Torah came during the twilight years of his life. We know from Acts 7:23 that Moses was forty years old when he tried to liberate the Hebrews his way by murdering an Egyptian who was abusing a fellow Hebrew. When his approach failed, he fled Egypt and traveled to the land of Midian, which was south of Canaan and may have been in Arabia east of the Gulf of Aqabah.¹¹ He was there forty years before the Lord appeared to him in a burning bush and commissioned him to return to Egypt to lead the Hebrews out of slavery and into a new land (7:23–34). This would place Moses as the leader of liberation at age eighty in the year 1446. So over the next forty years of his life, from age eighty to one hundred twenty years old, he led the Hebrews in the wilderness and wrote the Torah. God saw Moses' final forty years as prime time for what he wanted to do through him.

 EXPERIENCE GOD'S HEART

- *If you are older, perhaps retired, and living your twilight years, what does God's work through Moses tell you about what God can still do through you? Take some time right now to come before the Lord and commit your future to him. Also ask him to grant you all that you need to do the work he lays out for you.*

- *If the twilight years of your life are still a long way off, what can you infer from Moses' life about God's patient work in your life? Is there still time for the Lord to prepare you and operate through you to accomplish whatever he has for you to do? Are you willing to receive his direction and follow his lead? Are you doing that now? Go to him. Lay yourself bare before him. Open your heart and mind to his. Dedicate yourself and your ways to him.*

First Readers

Given when Genesis was composed, its first readers would have been the liberated Hebrews and their immediate descendants. The Bible's opening book was written by God's prophet (Moses) for God's people on their way to becoming his nation in the Middle East.

Still, like all the books of the Bible, Genesis' first readers were never intended to be its only readers. Genesis is for all of God's people and is useful for "instruction and correction" so every believer can grow up in the way, the truth, and the life and become "fully mature and perfectly prepared to fulfill any assignment God" has for them (2 Timothy 3:16–17).

- *As you work through the rest of this study guide on Genesis, remain open to what God wants to teach you through it and be willing to cooperate with his Spirit to apply that instruction to your life. Make that commitment to God now, even putting it in writing below.*

Literary Type

Although Genesis reveals the creation of the heavens and the earth, it is not a scientific book. It speaks into biology, geography, and other disciplines of study and does so truly and accurately, but it is not a substitute for these subject areas. Instead, Genesis is first and foremost a work of history divinely inspired.

One indication of its historical nature is a recurring phrase in the Hebrew: "These are the generations of." This phrase occurs eleven times in Genesis, and in every instance except for one, it refers to human persons.

2:4   "This is the account [*toledot*] of the heavens and the earth."

5:1   "So here is the family history [*seper*] of Adam."

6:9   "This is the story [*toledot*] of Noah."

10:1   "This is the story [*toledot*] of the descendants of Noah's three sons."

11:10   "These are the descendants [*toledot*] of Shem."

11:27   "Here are the descendants [*toledot*] of Terah."

25:12   "This is the account [*toledot*] of the descendants of Abraham's son Ishmael."

25:19   "This is how the story [*toledot*] of Isaac begins."

36:1   "Here are the descendants [*toledot*] of Esau."

36:9   "This is the account [*toledot*] of Esau."

37:1   "This is the story [*toledot*] of the family of Jacob."

The Hebrew word *toledot* "refers to what is produced or brought into being by someone, or follows therefrom."[12]

These repeated phrases (what Bible scholars also refer to as formulas) (1) may introduce family histories and family stories or (2) may indicate the end of those accounts or (3) may tell about what became of the family line already mentioned.[13] The only part of Genesis that seems to lack the *toledot* formula is Joseph's story. Some scholars conclude from this and other evidence that Moses actually wrote the Joseph story (37:2b–50:26) and then compiled and edited the other family stories.[14] We know that Moses wove material from other source books into parts of the Torah. For example, Genesis 5:1 uses the Hebrew word for "book," *seper*, to indicate from where the family history of Adam came.[15] Another source mentioned and used is "the Book of the Wars of the Lord" (Numbers 21:14 NASB). So it may be that the *toledot* sections indicate other sources that Moses used to organize and write the histories we have in Genesis. Whether that's so or not, what these recurring *toledot* lines indicate is that Genesis presents what God wanted us to know about certain human families that actually lived, related to him, and died here on planet earth. In other words, Genesis is history, not myth or legend. So we should approach Genesis as historical narrative—read it and interpret it that way.

- *As we'll see, the family histories in Genesis display the ups and downs of life in a broken world: triumph and tragedy, integrity and deceit, generosity and greed, hope and despair, faith and doubt, dedication to God and dedication to self. What does your family history show?*

 SHARE GOD'S HEART

Our God is a Redeemer, filled with mercy and grace. He can work through even one family member to bring salvation to the rest of the family or repair their damaged relationships.

- *Will you be God's conduit of grace and mercy in your family? You can show God's redeeming heart through your actions or explain it through your words. Whatever he guides you to do in your family, your best witness will always be you: who you are, the attitudes you have, what you show you really care about, how you conduct yourself, especially when life is hard. Remain open to God for how you can bring grace and mercy into your family. If you are already doing this, note below how your efforts have been received so far. If you haven't done this yet, indicate what challenges you face and then ask the Lord to show you ways to overcome them.*

Talking It Out

Since Christians grow in community, not just in solitude, every "Talking It Out" section contains questions you may want to discuss with another person or in a group. Here are the exercises for this lesson.

1. Genesis is a book of origins, of firsts, that God wanted us to know about. Why do you think origins matter? What is it about beginnings that help us in the here and now and even into the there and not yet?

2. God made sure that Moses received the preparation he needed to fulfill his role as writer of the Torah. What is your role in life right now? Most of us have several roles to fulfill at once, from what we do in our families to what we engage in at school or at work or with friends and colleagues. Choose one of the roles you now have. What would you say has prepared you for it? Remember, preparation doesn't fulfill all we will face, but it does give us essential resources for dealing with whatever comes up.

3. Families matter to God, but none of them are perfect. In fact, family life is often messy. How would you describe your family? Who among your family knows and follows the God of the Bible? In what ways would you say their lives differ from the lives of other family members? How are their lives similar? Are there any family members you have been drawn to emulate? Explain your answer.

LESSON 2

The Purpose and Themes of Genesis

The purpose of Genesis is to give us God's revelation on origins. We don't have to guess where the universe and first life came from or wonder about essentials regarding human beginnings, human nature, human purpose and meaning, and the most significant trajectory of human history. Genesis provides critical insight on the goodness of creation and how it became corrupted. It tells us that the rebellion against God won't have the last word, that someone will come from Eve's descendants who will defeat evil. In fact, the *toledot* sections concerning human beings trace "God's program of bringing the seed of the Serpent under the dominion of the elect seed of the woman."[16] The serpent will not be the victor in history; God will! Genesis does not give us a complete history of early humanity, nor does it tell us everything we might like to know about the universe's early history. But the book gives us a divinely inspired and authoritative account of creation, first life, humanity's uniqueness, purpose, and meaning, how and why things went awry, and that God's plan is not to leave us on our own mired in our sin. Instead, his plan is to deliver us, bless us, and graciously give us an incredible future that we could never bring about on our own. God has given us a historical record we can understand and trust.

Given the book's first readers, Genesis also "supplies the historical basis for God's covenant with His people."[17] As the first book of the Torah, Genesis shows God's selection of Abraham, his covenant with this man, and his "promise to make [Abraham's] offspring into the people of God and to give them the land of Canaan as an everlasting inheritance."[18] Consequently, Genesis supplies "an indispensable prologue to the drama that unfolds in Exodus."[19] Moses supplies in Genesis what the Hebrews, Abraham's descendants, needed to know about God and his faithfulness and his overarching plan to bless them in a new land so they could thrive there and become a blessing to "all the families of the earth" (Genesis 12:3).

- *What do you need to know right now about God and his faithfulness and plan that would encourage you, inspire you, comfort you...in short, bless you?*

Key Themes

Several key themes emerge from the pages of Genesis.

Origins

As we have already mentioned, Genesis contains a number of firsts or beginnings. These are the beginnings that God has deemed the most important for us to know as we start our journey to understand him, to deepen our trust in him, and to keep committing ourselves to living life his way.

- *Revisit that list of origins at the beginning of Lesson 1. Which ones are you most interested in? Why?*

The Land

Land also plays a critical role in Genesis. In chapter 1, God rolls back the waters of the deep to let dry land appear (1:9–10). After he creates Adam, he places him in a beautiful and already fruitful garden to begin his life on earth (2:8–15). When God comes to Abraham, his covenant to bless him and his descendants, and through them to bless all the other families of the earth, includes a land promise (12:1–3; 13:14–17; 15:7, 18–21).

God wants his people to have a place to live and to thrive, and Genesis shows this.

- *God cares about the spiritual aspects of our lives, and he also cares about our physical needs. In Genesis, these two sides of us—the spiritual and the physical—are tied together. Are you in need? What are your physical needs? Do you need land on which to live? Do you need food or clothing or a roof over your head? Whatever your needs, list them here.*

- *Now don't be shy about your needs. Let them be known to the body of Christ, the church. God works through his people most often. Give them the privilege of helping you and then remain open to how they choose to do that, with you receiving their gifts as coming from God's hand.*

♥ SHARE GOD'S HEART

Genuine faith always produces good and loving fruit, including when it comes to meeting people's physical needs. In the New Testament, James writes: "Your calling is to fulfill the royal law of love…: 'You must love and value your neighbor as you love and value yourself!'" (James 2:8). And that includes clothing those who lack clothing and feeding those who lack food. We can't do this for everyone, but we can do it for those we know, our neighbors, anyone close enough for us to know their needs (see 2:14–17; cf. Matthew 25:31–46).

- *Is there anyone in your circle of relationships who has physical needs you have the means to meet? It may require supplying life essentials such as offering food and clothing, or providing for financial needs such as paying an overdue bill, or meeting medical needs such as finding a specialist and perhaps covering the cost of the initial visit. Perhaps you have a vehicle you can loan or giveaway. Or maybe just some of your time, attention, and skills are the gifts to give. Whoever the person is and whatever the need, if you can address it, do it—and sooner rather than later.*

The Seed

Another important theme in Genesis is seed. In Genesis 1:11, "plants...bear seeds of their own kind, and every variety of fruit tree, each with power to multiply from its own seed." Seeds bear within them life that can produce fruit to sustain life and bring about new life. In 3:15, after the sin of Adam and Eve, God tells the tempter that he "will place great hostility between you and the woman [Eve], and between her seed and yours." The tempter's seed bears within it greater sin and death, but Eve's seed will one day bring the Life-Giver who will crush the head of the tempter, dealing him a fatal blow that will one day put an end to his rebellion while bringing the promise of full and ultimate redemption to Eve's seed. And then in Genesis 22, in response to Abraham's obedience, God tells him, "I will greatly bless you! I will make sure your seed becomes as numerous as the stars of heaven and as the sand of the seashore...the entire world will be blessed through your seed" (vv. 16–18). The fruitfulness of life will come to Abraham and his seed, his descendants.

Everyone is a descendant of someone. Every human life begins as part of another. This is the way God has established how his creation is to work.

• *Who gave you earthly life? Write their names below.*

• *What are or were your parents like?*

• *Did they bless your life? If so, in what ways?*

• *If they routinely caused you harm, what did you learn from them about how not to be, and what steps have you taken to live differently? (This is one way to redeem your past. We'll encounter other ways later in this study.)*

Blessed to Be a Blessing

In the "Introduction" to Genesis in The Passion Translation, Brian Simmons speaks to this theme:

> Blessing is perhaps the most important theological "glue" that holds Genesis together and connects it to the rest of the Hebrew Scriptures. In Gen. 1, God blesses humans (1:22, 28), and then they lose that blessing (ch. 3). God returns to this theme again in Gen. 12, where he seeks to restore this blessing to humanity once more through choosing a couple, Abraham and Sarah, and their *zera*—their seed,

their offspring, their "nation." And this blessing is manifested in several lives, like Abraham's and Joseph's.

But what is this blessing?...A working definition is to "empower for abundant living in every sphere of life." This abundant-life empowerment flows from a vibrant relationship with God. When God blesses you, your life will soar into his abundance! This blessed, abundant life includes being fruitful (reproduction) and multiplying (increasing in number) (1:25); equal empowerment for both men and women to live on this planet (1:28); an infusion of power and favor to succeed in life (5:1–2); a relationship with the God of the universe (17:6); prosperity, abundance, and success (39:2). And yet, Yahweh's blessing was never an end in and of itself. We were always meant to leverage our abundant life for the sake of the world—we are blessed to be a blessing![20]

- *Write down up to four things God has blessed you with. This can include a spiritual gift, a natural talent, a material possession, a relationship, a particular success... whatever it is, record it below.*

- *Now consider how you can share with others at least two of those blessings in the coming weeks. You have been blessed to be a blessing, so act on that truth.*

Faith in God and His Promises

Many of the believers mentioned in the great Hall of Faith presented in Hebrews 11 come from the stories of God's people revealed in Genesis.

- *Below you'll find the list of individuals the writer of Hebrews points to as examples of faith whose stories are told in Genesis. Select any four from the list to see what Hebrews says about them, and then jot down your findings next to their names:*

Abel (Hebrews 11:3–4)

Enoch (v. 5)

Noah (v. 7)

Abraham and Sarah (vv. 8–12, 17–19)

Isaac (v. 20)

Jacob (v. 21)

Joseph (v. 22)

- *What would you conclude about faith from these examples?*

- *Notice what the writer of Hebrews infers from the Hall of Faith examples (vv. 1–2, 6, 13–16, 39–40). What would you add to your thoughts about faith as a result of reading these passages?*

 EXPERIENCE GOD'S HEART

The most basic trait of faith is trust.

Do you trust God?

Do you trust his Word, the Bible?

Trust goes beyond mere belief *that* God will do what he has promised and *that* he's telling the truth. Trust believes *in* who God is, *in* what he has promised, and *in* the truths he reveals. People of faith give themselves over to God, rely on him, embrace him, love him with all they are and have. They trust that he has their best interests at heart and that he will not abandon them, no matter the cost they might pay for placing their faith in him.

- *Describe the faith you have in God, his promises, and his truth-soaked revelation. Is your faith strong or weak, full-hearted or half-hearted, steady or shaky?*

- *Where do you need to shore up your faith? What do you believe you need to do to bring greater confidence and maturity to your faith commitment to the Lord?*

- *Take some time to be still before the Lord and then ask him to help you develop your faith in him. He will always honor this request.*

Beginning of God's Redemptive Plan

Genesis records the first human sin and God's response to it (Genesis 3). Human corruption doesn't mark the end of God's work. Instead, it evokes Yahweh's work of redemption. He refuses to give up on his image bearers! He sets a plan in motion that will overcome sin and its devastating consequences.

- *More details about God's plan of salvation will come out later in our study. For now, take some time to acknowledge before the Creator-Savior what he has done to deliver you from sin and death. Thank him for his gracious work in your life.*

History's Foundation

Genesis opens up to us history from God's vantage point. It provides *the* foundational perspective of humanity's past. It tells us where we came from, what and who we are, why things are not the way they are supposed to be, and what God has initiated to save us from our own corruption. God reveals to us what he wants us to know, and this shows us that he has always been reaching out to us, calling us back to him so we can find genuine and everlasting fulfillment in him. So let's delve into this foundational book to discover what the Creator and Savior wants us to know.

Talking It Out

1. Among the key themes that are developed in Genesis, which one(s) is most important to you right now in your life? Why is this so?

2. What are two or three promises that God makes in Scripture that you have relied on? Share some examples of his fulfillment of these promises in your life. How has God keeping his word to you impacted your faith in him?

3. History matters to God. The Christian faith is founded on fact not fantasy, on history not mythology. What about the history recorded in Scripture do you know? What of church history have you learned? What are some steps you can take to learn biblical and church history to find out how you can live as a result of the lessons they teach?[21]

LESSON 3

In the Beginning

(1:1–25)

If you've ever read *The Lord of the Rings* trilogy by J. R. R. Tolkien or watched the movies that put large segments of those books on film, you know that Tolkien must have spent a lot of time and creative energy coming up with the world his books describe. He tells us about a land called Middle Earth with such territories as Rohan, Gondor, and Eriador and rivers named Anduin, Baranduin, and Forest River and mountains called The Lonely Mountain, Grey Mountains, and Ephel Durath (Mountains of Shadow). Tolkien created places of beauty, such as the Shire and Rivendell; places of protection, such as Helm's Deep; and places of danger and evil, such as Mordor. Various creatures populated Middle Earth, including hobbits, dwarfs, elves, wizards, humans, Ringwraiths, ents, orcs, and trolls. Tolkien even created languages and histories for his various creatures. It took at least seventeen years for him to write this incredible series of fiction, and even after that, he was still tweaking the story of his fantasy world.[22] Tolkien proved himself a master storyteller.

As great a writer as Tolkien was, he had a variety of tools at his disposal. He was an expert in philology, a professor of English language and literature, and an active member of a group known as The Inklings, which included a number of prominent intellectuals and writers, among whom was C. S. Lewis. Tolkien had a great deal going for him, all of which helped prepare him and even inspire him to write the high level of fiction found in *The*

Lord of the Rings. Tolkien is admired far and wide for his literary achievements. And he should be.

Now, let's consider God. What did he have available to him when he created the entire universe? Nothing outside of himself! Initially, he had no materials to work with, no prior experience creating, no plans of others to consult. All God had was himself—his own knowledge, wisdom, power, mind, will, vision, and goodness. From him, and him alone, the whole created order came to be. That's simply staggering! We have nothing to compare that to. All human creations start with something already available—no exceptions. But God had no one and nothing to help him create what he did. All he had was who and what he is.

Fortunately, God has given us his record of what he did. He provides a glimpse into his amazing creative activity at the very beginning. Let's explore this divine account.

First Things First

Genesis appropriately begins with the start of everything. Its content comes *before* the first *toledot* section of the book, covering from 1:1–2:3. We might call this the prologue of Genesis.

The opening words of the Bible are "When God created the heavens and the earth" (1:1). The word translated "when" here is actually a phrase in Hebrew, *bereshit*, literally "in the beginning." Bible commentator Gordon J. Wenham says that this refers to "the beginning of time itself, not to a particular period within eternity."[23] In other words, God's initial act of creation began time. There was no time before time began, just the timeless, eternal God. Wrap your head around that truth! So the moment God created the heavens and the earth, time started. (See Appendix 1, "The Big Bang and Genesis," for the scientific support of an absolute beginning for the physical universe.)

Genesis 1:1 concisely tells us what God did first: he created the entire natural universe. The explicit focus here is on the physical world: matter, space, and time. We know from other passages, however, that he also created the supernatural world—a world of spirit beings.

• *Look up the following passages and jot down what they tell you about God's creation work:*

Nehemiah 9:6

Psalm 148:2–5

Colossians 1:16

When God speaks to Job, he tells him that "all the angels shouted for joy" when he, God, "laid the earth's foundation'" (Job 38:7, 4 NIV). This indicates that the angels were created before the earth and witnessed God's creative handiwork as he established it. What this suggests is that God's creation of the heavens and the earth includes the physical, visible world *and* the spiritual, invisible world—the world of nature and the world of supernature. Genesis 1 and 2 do not explicitly reveal that God created the angelic world, but when we compare other biblical passages to the opening creation account, there is no question that God created all things that exist outside of himself, including the spiritual beings called angels.

Genesis 1:1 also tells us that *God* did this creation work. No one other than God is mentioned. He is the One who brought everything else into existence. The Bible is clear on this.

- *Check out the passages that follow and write down what they teach about God as the Creator:*

  Isaiah 42:5

  Isaiah 44:24

  Isaiah 45:11–12, 18

  John 1:1–3

  Colossians 1:15–17

  Revelation 4:11

So God's first act of creation was to bring into existence the entire universe, physical and spiritual. The word translated "created" in Genesis 1:1 is the Hebrew term *bara*, "which is used in the Old Testament exclusively for God's creativity, things that only God can do."[24] What is it here that only God can do? *Only he can bring something into being from nothing.* This is called creation *ex nihilo*, "out of nothing." God is and always has been. Then he makes something that wasn't there at all, and he makes it without using anything other than his own mind, will, and power.

By itself, the term *bara* does not require creation from nothing. But in Genesis 1, no mention is made of God creating the entire universe out of anything that already existed, and other passages make it clear that he made the universe by his word alone, with "alone" implied.

- *What do the following passages tell you about how God created the heavens and the earth?*

    Psalm 33:6, 9

    Psalm 148:1–5

    Hebrews 11:3

Now when God initially created the universe, it did not pop into existence fully ordered.

- *What was the condition of the earth according to Genesis 1:2?*

 WORD WEALTH

Four key terms appear in Genesis 1:2 that unlock the rest of the creation account: *formless*, *empty*, *darkness*, and *the deep*. The Hebrew word for "formless" is *tohu*, and it means "unformed, unshaped." The word translated "empty" is *bohu*, and it signifies uninhabited. When used together they indicate complete disorder, chaos, disorganization, a waste place.[25] "Darkness" is the word *kosheck*, which indicates the absence of light, and "the deep," *hamayin tehom*, refers to unorganized waters.

Combined, these four words tell us that the initial condition of earth was dreadful. It was a primeval, drenched, chaotic wasteland, unsuitable for life. But God would not leave it in this state. The rest of the creation account shows how God formed the formless, filled what was empty, brought light to penetrate the darkness, and set boundaries on the deep waters so land could appear.

EXPERIENCE GOD'S HEART

Disorganization, disorder, chaos, and the like are often characteristics of the creative process. Inventors, artists, writers, musicians, and numerous other individuals who create know this. The road to beauty, to great artistry, to incredible effectiveness is usually bumpy and messy, at least during parts of the journey. God performed the greatest creative achievement imaginable, and yet it didn't pop into existence absolutely perfect, with nothing else needed to achieve his goals for it.

- *Regardless of your vocation, you likely have times you need to be—even want to be—creative in it. You want to bring order out of disorder, effectiveness out of ineffectiveness, utility out of brokenness, beauty out of ugliness. Reflect on how our universe began and realize that you are doing Creator-like work. Your desires find their source in him. Meditate on this, and then turn to the Master Craftsman and ask him to aid you in the creative process and goals. You won't find a better resource than him!*

The Days of Creation

Genesis 1 peels back the curtain of eternity and reveals what the Creator does after producing the initial substance of his brand-new work. Amidst the chaos, "God's Spirit" is present, hovering "over the face of the waters" (v. 2). The Holy Spirit is ready for action, and that action comes with incredible power, infinite knowledge and wisdom, and full control over creation.

- *As you read through Genesis 1:3–2:3, jot down under each numbered day what God did on that day.*

DAY 1   **DAY 4**

DAY 2   **DAY 5**

DAY 3   **DAY 6**

- *What do you notice between Days 1 and 4? How do the events on these days relate to each other?*

- *What about the correlations between Days 2 and 5? What are they?*

- *Now consider Days 3 and 6. How do the events on those days relate to each other?*

Some Bible scholars view the days of Genesis as chronological: Day 1, then Day 2, then Day 3, and so on. Other scholars see the correspondence between Days 1 and 4, 2 and 5, and 3 and 6 and conclude that perhaps the creation events occurred in that order or that they at least show the sophisticated literary structure of the creation narrative.[26] (For more on the Hebrew word for "day," which is *yom*, see Appendix 2, "The Length of Days.") When we lay out the correspondence between the Days, we find the following:

1. God penetrates the darkness with light (Day 1) and creates the luminaries to govern the day and the night (Day 4).

2. God creates the sky and seas (Day 2) and then populates them with creatures that can reproduce their own kind (Day 5).

3. God creates dry land and vegetation (Day 3) and populates the earth with land animals and humans, also giving these creatures the ability to reproduce their own kind (Day 6).

More connections can be seen when we consider the four key words of 1:2 and their relationship to the six days described in the creation account:
Genesis 1:2 – "The earth was completely formless (*tohu*) and empty (*bohu*), with nothing but darkness (*kosheck*) draped over the deep (*hamayin tehom*)."

Formless (*tohu*)	Empty (*bohu*)	Darkness (*kosheck*)	Draped over the deep (*hamayin tehom*)
Unformed, unshaped	Empty, uninhabited	Dark, no light	Unorganized waters, the deep
▼	▼	▼	▼
To be shaped	To be inhabited	To be enlightened	To be organized
▼	▼	▼	▼
Geographic forms, land masses	Kinds of life	Light and light-bearers	Major areas of water

- *What do these literary traits indicate about Moses'
  writing abilities?*

- *What do these creation activities reveal about God's
  ability and knowledge to bring order out of disorder,
  fulfillment to emptiness, and light to darkness?*

- *Since God did this with the natural world, do you think he can do it in your life? Explain your answer.*

💚 SHARE GOD'S HEART

There are at least two ways in which we come close to creating as God does. One way is to come up with an idea for a product or process and then turn that mental picture into a brick-and-mortar reality. The other way is to take something that's disorganized and organize it, or ineffective and make it effective, or ugly and turn it into a thing of beauty, or lifeless and bring it to life. Once we have created, the other God-like thing we can do is to share it.

- *Write out some things or processes you know you can create.*

- *Now choose at least one of them to create in the coming days—not to create for yourself but for someone else. Create to give it away, to share it, as God has done with his creative work.*

Talking It Out

1. Between God and the universe, God was first. And when he created the universe, all that it is came into existence: time, space, and matter. None of these properties or their characteristics existed before God made them. This reveals that God is radically different from the physical universe. Since the physical universe is temporal, God must be timeless. The universe is spatial, so God must be spaceless. The universe is material (physical), which means that God must be immaterial (non-physical or pure spirit). What are other characteristics does the universe have that God doesn't?

2. Isaiah reveals: "This is what Yahweh says, heaven's Creator, who alone is God. He created the earth, shaped it, and established it all by himself. He made it fit and orderly...[He did not create it a chaos] for its inhabitants" (Isaiah 45:18).[27] Throughout Genesis 1, God forms the formless and fills what's empty. He brings order out of disorder. What can you do to bring greater order into your life and the lives of those around you?

3. Are there any truths that Genesis 1 reveals that surprised you or struck you more forcefully than they have before? If so, which ones, and why did they affect you that way?

God's Image Bearers

(1:26–2:3)

If you ever wondered whether God cares about us, Genesis 1 should put that question to rest. The first five days of creation lead to the climatic work of God's creative activity: the creation of humankind on Day 6. There he makes something truly unique among all else he has made, and he designs his final creation to be like him:

> Then God said, "Let us make a man and
> a woman in our image to be like us. Let
> them reign over the fish of the sea, the birds
> of the air, the livestock, over the creatures
> that creep along the ground, and over the
> wild animals." So God created man and
> woman and shaped them with his image
> inside them. In his own beautiful image,
> he created his masterpiece. Yes, male and
> female he created them. (vv. 26–27)

And with these words, God establishes a unique connection between him and us—one that begins with who he is, the One we have been created to image.

The Trinity

There, for the first time in Genesis, God refers to himself as "us": "Then God said, 'Let *us* make a man and a woman in *our* image to be like *us*'" (1:26, emphasis added). In the earlier verses, God commands and acts with no mention of anyone except him. But in verse 26, God refers to "us." Whom is God talking about? The oldest Jewish understanding is that God is indicating the heavenly court of angels, an idea that certainly has merit in other biblical passages (e.g., see 1 Kings 22:19–22; Job 1:6; 38:4–7; Psalm 89:5–6). But nowhere does Scripture say that human beings are made in anyone's image other than God's. We are not image bearers of God *and* angels, just of God.

With the fuller revelation given to us in the New Testament, the early Christians began to understand the "us" of Genesis 1:26 to be an implicit reference to the one God's deliberation within himself, specifically to the deliberation of the Father, the Son, and the Spirit. This is highly significant.

- *The Bible reveals that there is just one God, not many. Look up the following passages and write down what they tell you about God:*

Deuteronomy 6:4

Isaiah 43:10–13

Isaiah 44:6, 8

Isaiah 45:18

- *Now while the Bible teaches that there is just one God, it also reveals that God is the Father, the Son, and the Spirit. Look up each passage that follows and record what you find there about God as the Father or God as the Son or God as the Spirit:*

  2 Samuel 23:1–3

  John 1:1–3, 14

  John 6:27

Acts 5:1–4

1 Corinthians 8:4–6

Titus 2:13

Hebrews 10:15–16

2 Peter 1:1–2

1 John 5:20

- *Some biblical passages also present all three persons—*
  Father, Son, and Spirit—referring to them in such a way
  as to affirm all three as deity all at the same time. Here
  are some of the passages that mention the Father, the
  Son, and the (Holy) Spirit together, all involved in an
  interrelated way. Jot down next to each passage what
  you find there about this plurality in God and their
  activity.

Matthew 3:16–17

Matthew 28:18–20

Luke 1:35

2 Corinthians 13:14

The oneness of God and, at the same time, plurality within God led the church to formulate its most distinctive teaching—the Trinity. This doctrine affirms that God is three distinct, coequal, and coeternal persons who coexist in the same divine essence or nature and share all the same divine attributes. Put more briefly, God is one in his nature but three in his personhood. God's nature is *what* he is: for example, God is all-loving, all-powerful (omnipotent), all-knowing (omniscient), all-good (omnibenevolent), eternal (timeless), and unchanging (immutable). These aspects of his nature are called attributes, properties, characteristics, or perfections. They are all essential traits of what God is, of his nature or being.

Now this one God consists of three persons: Father, Son, and Spirit. God's personhood is about *who* he is. A person has the abilities to think, will, and feel. Each of the divine persons has these abilities in complete and perfect harmony. They are the truly perfect society!

So the Christian doctrine of the Trinity teaches that God has one nature with three centers of personhood. Put another way, God is three Whos coexisting in one What.

Let's go back to Genesis 1:26, which says, "Let *us* make a man and a woman in *our* image to be like *us*" (emphasis added). Who is "us" here? It is the one God—Father, Son, and Spirit—expressing their agreed-upon free choice to create the first human beings.

One analogy that often helps with understanding the Trinity comes from the nature of love. John says that God is love (1 John 4:16). Love involves three elements: a lover, a loved one, and a bond of love between them. The Father is the lover, the Son is the loved one, and the Spirit is the bond of love between the Father and the Son. Love is personal; only persons love. And in the case of the Trinity, the three divine persons not only love but are also the essence of love itself. Since they already eternally enjoyed the fullness of love between them, they chose to create, not out of loneliness but in order to share their love with what they made. And this love has been poured out most profusely on us, their image bearers.[28]

- *The personal God created personal beings, us, to image him, and he did this out of his love. What difference do you think this should make in how you relate to God, to yourself, and to fellow image bearers? (Keep in mind that God's love is active; it's focused on doing what is good, whether the objects of his love deserve it or not; see Acts 14:15–17.)*

Image Matters

With the creation of human beings, God deliberates within himself ("Let us"), and he commits to making human beings "in our image to be like us" (Genesis 1:26). He doesn't say anything like this about any other living creatures, just us human beings. So what this image bearing is all about is essential to understanding who and what we are. Let's focus in on all the key words used in Genesis 1:26–28 so we can learn what God says about us and then apply those truths.

Create (bara)

The word translated "created" three times in 1:27 is the Hebrew word *bara*, which is always used of God's activity in Scripture, and it indicates the initiation of something new and unique that God is doing. Humanity is his special work, unique creatures among all the ones he created.

Man (adam)

In the original Hebrew of Genesis 1:26, it reads "Let us make man as our image." The word *man* here is *adam*, and it occurs without the definite article "the." This means that *adam* here refers to humanity in general, not to a specific human being. In the context of Genesis 2, humanity began with one man and one woman, Adam and Eve.

Image (selem)

The Hebrew term translated "image" in Genesis 1:26 and 27 is *selem*, and it refers to a work of art, a statue, or an object standing for or symbolizing something else. It's usually used in the Old Testament to designate idols, physical representations of false gods (Daniel 3:1–7; Habakkuk 2:18–19). In the Septuagint, which is the oldest Greek translation of the Old Testament, the Greek word *eikon* is used for the Hebrew *selem*, and *eikon* means "icon." The apostle Paul uses this word when he writes about people who exchanged "the unfading splendor of the immortal God to worship the fading image of other humans, idols [*eikon*] made to look like people, animals, birds, and even creeping reptiles" (Romans 1:23). In 1 Corinthians 11:7, Paul refers back to man's creation and says that man "*is* the portrait [*eikon*] of God" (emphasis added), not "is *in* God's image." Put another way, there's not something just inside of us that is God's image. Instead, we, our very essence, what makes us human, *is* the very image of God.[29]

An image is not the original, but it bears a resemblance to the original and represents it.[30] When we see statues and paintings of famous people, we know they are not actually those people but resemble and represent them. Moreover, the art itself reveals truths about the artists who made them (for example, their artistic style, materials they like to use, and the quality of their abilities). Likewise, we represent and resemble the divine Artist who made us.

An image can also be alive or lifeless. Seth was a *living* image of Adam (Genesis 5:3), and all human beings are living images of the living God. We are unlike the lifeless materials of wood, stone, and metal that people have used to form images of false, lifeless gods.

An image, which is typically visible, can stand for what is invisible. The New Testament reveals that this is the case with Jesus Christ. Jesus is the visible image of the invisible God (Colossians 1:15; 2 Corinthians 4:4). As a man, he images God as we do, yet perfectly and without sin. As God, he images deity to us. Like the writer of Hebrews says, "The Son is the dazzling radiance of God's splendor, the exact expression of God's true nature—his mirror image" (Hebrews 1:3). When we look into the face of Jesus, we not only see us as we should be, but we also see the very character of God made visible: his love, goodness, grace, mercy, intelligence, wisdom, kindness, power, and the like. God is at work in those of us who trust in Christ to conform us to "the likeness [eikon] of his Son" (Romans 8:29). In fact, we are "continually being renewed into the likeness [eikon] of the One who created [us]" (Colossians 3:10).

Like (demut)

In Genesis 1:26, God says he will create human beings as his image and his likeness. This likeness idea comes from the Hebrew word demut, and it suggests similarity, resemblance, and correspondence. When Adam fathers his son, Seth, the text says that Adam "fathered a child in his own likeness [demut]" (5:3). Seth was not identical to Adam, but he did resemble him in significant ways.

Male and Female (zakar, neqeba)

"Male and female he created them" (1:27). The Hebrew terms for "male" and "female" refer to the sexual distinction between men and women.[31] The text moves from creating man (humanity) as God's image bearer to creating the image male and female. In other words, males and females are equally image bearers.

The man is not more of an image bearer than the woman or vice versa. Man bears the divine image as does woman.

Moreover, the fact that the Hebrew words bring to the forefront the sexual differences between men and women indicates that our bodies are part of the divine image. The Bible does not demean or ignore the human body. Rather, it exalts the body, including it as part of the divine image.

Notice, too, that God didn't create one human being to bear the image but two distinct human beings, the smallest number that can make a society, a social group. So just as God is a society of three, human beings, even of different sexes, can become a society and even enlarge their society and multiply the number of their societies. We were made to be social beings, not lone rangers, and it's in our social relationships that our divine image is enlarged and more fully fulfilled.

Putting It All Together

Now that we have all the pieces, let's see if we can put them together to see the picture the puzzle presents about us and some of its practical implications.

1. We are special and unique among all God has made.

- *Since you are God's special creation, how can this help you in developing your own self-image?*

2. We are God's image bearers. That is what we are, our very essence. Our humanness is the image of God.

• *Since your very humanness is the image of God, how do you represent him (that is, stand for him and reveal him to others)? And how do you resemble him (that is, how are you similar to God)?*

3. Since all human beings are divine image bearers, we have this fact about us in common.

• *Since you, your neighbor, your family members, and all other human beings you come in contact with are God's image bearers, how should this influence the way you treat them?*

4. Our bodies are included in our divine image.

• *Your body matters to God. Caring for it is important. And you're even to use it in your service to God, as Paul says: "I plead with you to give your bodies to God. Let them be a living sacrifice, holy—the kind he can accept" (Romans*

12:1 NLT). What should you do to care for your body? How can you use it to reveal and serve God?

5. Male and female are equally divine image bearers.

- *If you are a man, how do you regard women? Do you see them as your equals? If so, what does that look like in your life? If not, what changes do you need to make?*

- *If you are a woman, how do you regard the men around you? Do you treat them as your equals? If so, what does that look like in your life? If not, what changes do you need to make?*

- *God is a fully harmonious society of three persons co-existing in the same exact nature. Each human being, on the other hand, is one person existing in one nature, and we were created to be social beings (male and female), desiring and needing others like us. What do you do to cultivate relationships with others—such as family members, friends, work associates, fellow believers at church, and neighbors? Remember, you are blessed to bless others.*

6. We are living, visible images of the living, invisible God.

- *How are you revealing the invisible God to others? How does your life point people back to him?*

7. As image bearers of God, we are not equal to or exactly the same as God. We are like him, but we are not him. As the psalmist says, we have been "created only a little lower than Elohim" (Psalm 8:5); Elohim is one of the many names of God.

- *In the following chart, list attributes or activities of God that you know in the left-hand column. In the right-hand column, link corresponding attributes or activities that fit you. You will find that you share some attributes with God, though he has them infinitely, and all human beings have them finitely. Also, list some activities he performs that you don't and perhaps even can't. You'll find starting the chart some examples that should help you add to the lists.*

GOD...	I...
Knows everything	Know some things
Is perfect	Am imperfect
Created out of nothing	Make things from other things

Since no human being is God (with the lone exception being Jesus of Nazareth), how would you answer the following questions?

- *Who should receive my ultimate allegiance, God or man?*

- *Who has the greatest authority to speak into my life, God or man?*

- *Who knows me best and looks after my best interests the most, God or man?*

- *To whom, ultimately, do I owe my life and being, God or man?*

❤ SHARE GOD'S HEART

One of the best ways we can serve our fellow image bearers is to keep ourselves aligned with God and his ways. That is not just the best way for Christians to live, but it is the best way for everyone to live whether they believe in God or not. Yahweh is the one and only God; all other gods are false. He is the source of all that's good, beautiful, and true; nothing else even comes close. The universe is Christian, summed up in Christ who is all in all (Colossians 1:15–20). It is not Buddhist, Hindu, atheistic, pantheistic, or any other rival religious or philosophical worldview. So when we speak, write, love, work—no matter what we say, do, think, or feel—we, in some way, declare the truth about God, his world, and his image bearers. For this reason, we should heed Paul's admonition: "Let every activity of [our] lives and every word that comes from [our] lips be drenched with the beauty of our Lord Jesus, the Anointed One" (3:17). It is the truth and following its way that sets all people free (John 8:32; Galatians 5:1). So share God's heart by proclaiming him and his ways in all you are and do.

- *How do you currently proclaim him and his ways in your activities?*

- *What else can you do to further this revelation work in your life so others may see God in you?*

What Image Bearers Should Do

We were created for a purpose, blessed to be a blessing.

- *Read Genesis 1:28. What did God command his image bearers to do?*

- *Read the TPT notes for verse 28. What would you add to your above answer about God's command to his image bearers?*

- *What implications do you think this passage has on the way you should live your life? How can you be fruitful and bring dominion into your everyday life, your work, your thought life, and other sides to your life? Keep in mind that dominion does not entail lording yourself over others, an idea the Bible does not support (e.g., Luke 22:24–27; John 13:5–17). Nor does Scripture support abusing anything or anyone.*

- *God knew his image bearers as well as his other earthly creatures would need fuel to fulfill their purpose. What was that food to be initially (Genesis 1:29–30)?*

The Seventh Day: Pleasure and Rest

Several times in Genesis 1 God declares his delight in his own handiwork.

- *Read through 1:1–25 and below write what God said about his creation work and on what day he said it.*

- *Now read verse 31 and summarize what God said about all the creation work he achieved.*

- *Are you delighted by God's creation? Explain your answer.*

- *Do you find pleasure in the work that you do? Why or why not?*

- *Paul tells us that "we are to live our lives with pure hearts in the constant awe and wonder of our Lord God. Put your heart and soul into every activity you do, as though you are doing it for the Lord himself and not merely for others" (Colossians 3:22–24). Do you think that this approach to your work would change your perspective and attitude for the better? Explain your answer.*

After God finished his creative work, he who is all-powerful and unlimited in every other way did something remarkable.

- *According to Genesis 2:1–3, what did God do once his creation work was finished?*

• *Did God rest because he had become exhausted from creating? Read Isaiah 40:28–31. What does this passage tell you about God's energy level?*

• *Now read Matthew 11:28–30. What does Jesus promise those who come to him with their heavy burdens?*

God's rest on the seventh day is one of the justifications given for us to rest after our workweek.

• *Read Exodus 20:8–11. What comparison is made there between God's creation activity and subsequent rest and how the Hebrews were supposed to work and rest?*

- *What do Exodus 20:11 and Genesis 2:3 say about what God declared of the seventh day?*

Gordon Wenham writes:

> God is holy: holiness is the essence of his character. Anything else that is described as holy in the OT [Old Testament] derives its holiness from being chosen by God and given to him in the correct prescribed manner...The seventh day is the very first thing to be hallowed in Scripture, to acquire that special status that properly belongs to God alone. In this way Genesis emphasizes the sacredness of the Sabbath. Coupled with the threefold reference to God resting from all his work on that day, these verses give the clearest of hints of how man created in the divine image should conduct himself on the seventh day.[32]

The opening section of Genesis has, in Bible scholar Henri Blocher's words, "two peaks, mankind and the sabbath. This would be better expressed by saying that the creation of mankind crowns the work, but the sabbath is its supreme goal." Continuing he says that the Sabbath

> relativizes the works of mankind, the contents of the six working days. It protects

mankind from total absorption by the
task of subduing the earth, it anticipates
the distortion which makes work the sum
and purpose of human life, and it informs
mankind that he will not fulfil [sic] his
humanity in his relation to the world which
he is transforming but only when he raises
his eyes above, in the blessed, holy hour of
communion with the Creator.[33]

God creates his image bearers to engage in subduing the rest of the created order, to be his vice-regents on earth. And he commands his image bearers to reproduce and populate the earth provided for them (Genesis 1:28). But on the seventh day, God wants his image bearers to rest from their labors, to treat that day as sacred, recalling with gratitude what he has done for them. Work is good and God-given, but no matter how much we work, we will never master life. The Sabbath is a weekly reminder that life is a gift. We cannot earn it, no matter how hard or long we labor.[34]

 EXPERIENCE GOD'S HEART

• *Do you take time each week to rest? If not, why? How is that working out for you?*

- *Sometimes we "rest" in ways that exhaust us rather than remind us of God's gift of life, refuel us, and restore us. What are some things you do that give you genuine respite from your labors?*

- *Our rest should also lead us to raise our eyes to our Creator in thanksgiving and praise. Ultimately, we were made for him. Our tasks and achievements are secondary to who and what we are and who made us. Take some time out this week to turn toward the One in whose image you have been made, thank him for his many blessings, and praise him for who he is and what he does.*

Talking It Out

1. The Trinity is probably one of the hardest doctrines of the Christian faith to understand. What did you find in this lesson that helped you better grasp this biblical teaching? What still confuses you? What would you like to learn about the Trinity that hasn't been discussed here?

2. The fact that God is a unified and harmonious society of persons and we are his image bearers should inspire us to seek peaceful and productive ways to live together. Of course, for relationships to develop and flourish, we need common ground on which to build a foundation of mutual trust and cooperation. What are some common ground features of human life on which we can build even with those who are very different from us?

3. Jesus said that "the Sabbath was made for the sake of people, and not people for the Sabbath" (Mark 2:27). Relate that to Exodus 20:8–11 and 23:12. How do these passages support what Jesus said? And how does God's declaration about the seventh day's sacredness (Genesis 2:3) relate to Jesus' words and those found in Exodus?

LESSON 5

Adam and Eve in Paradise

(2:4–25)

Genesis 1 reveals God's creative work on a grand, cosmic scale, then turns to his overall work shaping and filling planet earth. Beginning in 2:4, the focus narrows even more, first to the condition of earth and then to more detail about God's creation of the first man and the first woman and the location he prepared for them and placed them to begin their new life together. Human life starts and flourishes in paradise.

The Narrative Flow

Genesis 2:4 introduces what will follow until the writer, Moses, moves into a new section starting with chapter 5, verse 1. From now on, we'll use the term "books" to refer to these *toledot* sections (family histories) and we'll number them. So the prologue of Genesis is where no *toledot* passage is found (1:1). Chapter 2, verse 4 is the first *toledot* passage, likely marking the start of a new section (2:4–4:26), which we'll call Book 1.

• *Read Genesis 2:4 and summarize what it says.*

- *Now read 5:1 and jot down its content focus here.*

- *Genesis 1:1 tells us what God initially did on a cosmic scale. Starting in 2:4, we learn more about God's creation activity on earth, especially as it concerns humanity's origins. Genesis 5:1 turns to Adam and Eve and their line of descendants and what they do. If you were to summarize or illustrate the different stages of focus that these three sections of Genesis have, what would you write or draw?*

The Garden Paradise and Beyond

Before we turn to the details surrounding the creation of Adam and Eve, let's turn our attention to the state of the earth as revealed in Genesis 2. What kind of place did God create for his image bearers to live and thrive in? Let's find out.

- *Read Genesis 2:5–20. Zero in on the environment in which humanity would and did reside. As you do, answer the following questions:*

  Was the entire earth full and lush with life, already fully developed, or was there life still to come? Provide support for your answer.

  Describe the special place God prepared for the first man and first woman.

  In what ways was the "garden paradise" for image bearers different from the land surrounding it?

  Read through the study notes in TPT for Genesis 2:10–14, focusing on the various meanings for the four rivers mentioned. What do these meanings tell you about the garden paradise and the water sources of life that God supplied?

 EXPERIENCE GOD'S HEART

- *God created a special place for the first human pair. Do you have a special place you like to go when you want to meet with God without interruptions, a place that reminds you what God is like and what he provides? If so, go to that place soon and seek his face. Rest in his presence, enjoying the peace you have with him through Jesus Christ. He is your Creator, Sustainer, and Savior. He accepts you just as you are while loving you so much that he won't leave you as you are. Relax in the knowledge that he always wants what's good for you.*

- *If you don't have a special place for meeting with God on occasion, we encourage you to find such a place. While God is always accessible to us, at times we need to pull away from life's demands in order to find rest and peace, including with him. Don't neglect your own needs. God supplied everything the first human beings needed, and he wants to do the same for you. Involve him in your search for a place of refreshment that you can use to rest in his presence.*

Humanity's Beginning

The primary focus of Genesis 2 is not land, rivers, trees, or animals for their own sake. Rather, it's the start of humankind,

God's image bearers. How did God make them? What did he provide for them? What were they supposed to do? What was their relationship to him, their Creator? And how did he relate to them? This chapter of Genesis answers these questions.

The First Man

- *Genesis 2:7 describes the creation of the first man. List the steps God took to make Adam.*

- *God could have just spoken man into existence. Instead, God took the time to shape him from earth he had already created and then breathed life into him. Why do you think God was so intimately involved in humanity's creation? What does this tell you about how he regards and relates to his image bearers?*

🅝 WORD WEALTH

In the first chapters of Genesis, the Hebrew words translated "living soul" in 2:7 and used to describe the first man are also used of animals (translated "life" in 1:20 and "living creature" in vv. 21 and 24). The differences between man as a living soul and that of animals are: (1) God breathes life directly into the first man but does not do this with animals; (2) God gives humanity authority over the animals, not animals authority over humans (1:29–30); and (3) God makes humanity as his image bearers, not so with the animals or any other creatures (1:26–27). We are God's unique and special creation. When he first made us, "The dust of earth and the breath of Deity mingled as one, so that Adam could interact in both realms (physical and spiritual). This breath or 'Spirit of life' was more than air; it brought intelligence, wisdom, light, and the image of God into Adam (see Job 32:8)."[35]

- *What did God do with Adam after he made him (Genesis 2:15)? What was Adam supposed to do there?*

- *Along with the tasks Adam was assigned, what did God tell him he could access for food, and what was he told to avoid and why?*

- *Adam's freedom was restricted on just one tree in Eden. What does this tell you about God's initial intention for humanity's use of his will? Did Adam have less freedom or more?*

DIGGING DEEPER

At the center of Eden were two trees: the Tree of Life and the Tree that gives the knowledge of good and evil. Bible commentators have proposed a number of interpretations regarding these trees. One point of debate has been over their physical reality. Some Bible scholars see the trees as real physical growths, with bark, leaves, and fruit. Other scholars see the trees as symbolic only, representing two paths or two choices God gave the first human beings: one of which led to life and the other that led to death. Since Eden was a real place with real physical sources of food, it seems best to regard these two trees as real physical entities that also served as symbols of the covenant God made with Adam. God provided him with everything he needed to live and flourish in the created world, but, along with the manifest realities of divine blessing, Adam would need to live with a limit. The fullness of life was his to enjoy, but one thing was forbidden—the tree designated as the Tree that gives the knowledge of good and evil. Everything else was available to him. Two real trees, two real choices.

So what was the knowledge of good and evil? Scholars have proposed several options.[36]

- One is that the knowledge of good and evil refers to discerning between what is morally right and what is morally wrong. But this view has been rejected because the very command to Adam that every source of food was available to him but one and that forbidden option would bring him death presupposes that he could already discern between right and wrong.

- Another option is that the knowledge of good and evil refers to sexual knowledge. The problem with this interpretation is that God commanded his image bearers to reproduce, which would require sexual knowledge, making that good knowledge to have (Genesis 1:28).

- A third view is that the knowledge of good and evil refers to moral omniscience (Genesis 3:5–6). The problem with this view is that "Though God enjoys omniscience, and the narrative suggests that the woman hoped to gain great knowledge (3:6), it is clear that the man and woman who ate the fruit did not acquire omniscience as a result, merely shame and a recognition of their nakedness (3:7–8)."[37]

- A fourth suggestion is that the Tree that gives the knowledge of good and evil, like the Tree of Life, simply describes the consequences of obeying or disobeying God's commandments. In this way the trees are like doors with signs posted on them—the signs indicating what lies beyond each door. While it's true that each tree offered different paths and consequences, this view doesn't seem to go far enough. The Tree of Life offered immortality (v. 22), not just a signpost to it. What, then, did the Tree that gives the knowledge of good and evil offer? It offered knowledge appropriate for God alone (vv. 5, 22).

- A fifth interpretive option sees the knowledge of good and evil as insight or wisdom. This seems to be the best choice. In 3:6, just before Eve eats from the forbidden tree, she notices that part of her draw to it was the "insight" she believed she would gain. In Scripture, wisdom brings insight, discernment, proper judgment, understanding, and the like. Of course, wisdom is something God wants us to have as the book of Proverbs makes clear. However, there is also "a wisdom that is God's sole preserve, which man should not aspire to attain (e.g., Job 15:7–9, 40; Prov 30:1–4), since a full understanding of God, the universe, and man's place in it is ultimately beyond human comprehension. To pursue it without reference to revelation is to assert human autonomy, and to neglect the fear of the Lord which is the beginning of knowledge (Prov 1:7)."[38] Rather than depend on God to learn the truth about the good and its ways, the Tree that gives the knowledge of good and evil represented a way to obtain this knowledge independently of God.[39]

Finally, virtually all Bible scholars have rejected the idea that the fruit of the Tree of Life and of the Tree that gives the knowledge of good and evil was magical. The fruit itself did not have the ability to convey ongoing life or moral wisdom. Both trees were real physical entities with real fruit, but neither contained magical qualities that could convey to partakers anything other than what other trees produce today. Rather, the Tree of Life, while a physical thing, also stood as a real symbol for the life that comes from God alone. And the Tree that gives the knowledge of good and evil was also a real tree that existed as a real symbol for the wisdom that comes only from God.

- *Can you think of other physical things in Scripture that were also symbols of deeper realities? List as many as you can below, including what they symbolized or represented.*

The First Woman

After Adam's creation, relocation, and divinely given charge, God commented about Adam's situation, added a specific task for the man to perform, and then supplied him with a partner without whom he would never have been able to fulfill God's creation mandates (Genesis 1:28–30).

- *What did God find to be unsuitable in Adam's situation in Paradise (2:18)?*

- *Since God's creative activity in Genesis 1 ends with his declaration that it all greatly pleased him (v. 31), what does his assessment of Adam's situation reveal about what creation day is being described in most of Genesis 2? Is it Day 1, Day 2, Day 3, Day 4, Day 5, or Day 6? Explain your answer.*

- *What did God want to do to remedy Adam's situation (v. 18)?*

- *Rather than informing Adam what was missing in his life, the Lord gave Adam a job to do that would help him discover what he still needed (vv. 18–20). What was that task? What does it show about Adam's relationship to the creatures in his environment?*

- *Read verses 21–23. What did God create to meet Adam's need, and how did he do it?*

- *Who presented the first woman to the first man?*

- *How did Adam respond to the female image bearer whom God created and designed for him (v. 23)?*

- *How did this first human couple view one another (v. 25)?*

- *What does their response to each other reveal about the human body? For example, did they see it as good or bad, as delightful or embarrassing? Support your answer.*

 THE BACKSTORY

Later in Genesis 3, Adam will actually name the first woman Eve (v. 20), but in 2:23 when he initially meets her, he calls her

"Woman, for she was taken from man." The Hebrew "word for man is *'ish*, and the word for woman is *'ishash*."[40] Notice "the play on words [here], which comes over only partially in the English 'man' and 'woman.'" Through this word play, the first man is expressing the common nature that he shares with the first woman. He immediately saw that she was like him, while also wonderfully different from him. What Adam says about her coming from his bones and his flesh also "affirms the family tie" linking them, which is yet another way to underscore what they have in common (Genesis 29:14; Judges 9:2; 2 Samuel 5:1; 19:12–13).[41] All of these comments are couched in poetic ecstasy. When Adam first encounters the Woman, he can't contain himself. He bursts into poetic praise and wonder.[42]

The fact that the first man needed one like him, that it was not good for him to be alone, shows that

> solitude contradicts the calling of humanity.
> From the very beginning, the human being
> is…a being-with; human life attains its full
> realization only in community. No man
> is an island, and everyone must discover
> himself to be his neighbour's neighbour.
> At the final completion of the operations
> of the grace of God, the multitude in the
> City of God multiplies the victory of the
> first couple over human solitude (Rev.
> 21–22). In the final paradise, as in the first,
> mankind will for ever be no longer alone.[43]

 WORD WEALTH

Notice, too, that God refers to the Woman he will make as "a suitable partner to be his [Adam's] help and strength" (Genesis 2:18). In a study note on this passage, the translator, Brian Simmons, points out that the key Hebrew word *'ezer* that refers to the Woman as "partner" is "frequently used for military help and ascribed to God himself fourteen times (e.g., Pss. 33:20; 54:4). It could be translated 'strong rescuer.'" When the word 'azar, from which 'ezer is derived, is used with the divine name, it forms proper names of God, such as Azarel ("God has helped"), Azriel ("My help is God"), and Azariah ("The Lord has helped"). In Deuteronomy 33, 'ezer is used of God to denote his strength and power in conjunction with his majesty and glory (vv. 26, 29).[44] So when the Woman is described as a "suitable partner" or helper, it does not designate subordination or weakness any more than God as our helper makes him subordinate to us. Instead it indicates that (1) the Woman is going to come after the man (the order of their creation), (2) she will correspond to the man (a true companion to him, one comparable to him), and (3) she will be strong and powerful in relationship to the man—namely, she will be his equal in strength or power. As Simmons concludes: "God's choice of the word 'ezer indicates that a man's wife is his first line of defense and an equal partner in the journey of life. The 'ezer is God's gift to the husband. The wife's role is more than that of an assistant to the man. She is the dynamic solution to man's loneliness as one who protects, reveals, and helps."[45]

❤ SHARE GOD'S HEART

In male-female relationships, sometimes one person treats the other as less than what God created him or her to be. Condescension, arrogance, self-centeredness, disinterest, forgetfulness, ignorance, bias, and a host of other attitudes and actions can lead us to mistreat those around us who have been made as God's image bearers.

- *Prayerfully and honestly search your heart to see if you have attitudes or have engaged in actions that tend to treat someone in your life as less than he or she is in God's sight. Work this matter through with God, recalling what the first two chapters of Genesis teach about man and woman.*

- *Now consider what you can do for this person that will demonstrate your renewed view of him or her as an equal divine image bearer. Then put your plan into action, even as soon as this week if you can.*

Marriage Then and Thereafter

Near the end of Genesis 2, the writer lays down principles for marriage based on the first marriage, the one between Adam and the Woman he will later name Eve. But nowhere does chapter 2 describe the first couple as married; instead their relationship as a married couple is assumed. Genesis 3, however, does indicate their marital relationship.

- *In the following verses from Genesis 3, record what you find that indicates that the first man and woman were married to each other.*

Verse 6:

Verse 8:

Verse 16:

Verse 17:

Verse 20:

- *Since the first human pair were married, who united them? See what Jesus said in Matthew 19:4–6.*

- *Based upon the first marriage, what are all subsequent marriages to be like (Genesis 2:24)?*

🛈 WORD WEALTH

The key components of marriage in Genesis 2:24 are described in the words "leaves," "attached," and "one flesh." Together they describe what God intended for marriage.

Leaving one's parents involves a shift in obligations. No longer is the man (or woman) primarily responsible for or to his parents. He leaves them in order to commit himself to another. This does not negate all responsibility to one's parents or the moral requirement to still honor them, but it does entail that they are no longer first in the man or woman's life. The marital bond supersedes the parental bond.

The attachment of the man to his wife is expressed by the Hebrew word *dabaq*, which means to cleave, to cling, to stick to or with. The term is used to describe bones that cling to skin (Job 19:20; Psalm 102:5), scales that cling to sea creatures (Job 41:23), and a tongue that clings to the roof of a dry mouth (Job 29:10). The term also "carries the sense of clinging to someone in affection and loyalty" (Genesis 34:3; Ruth 1:14).[46] The call to "unselfishly" attach oneself to one's wife conveys that marriage should be a permanent and loyal commitment to each other.

By leaving and attaching, man and woman in marriage become "one flesh." Two individuals voluntarily dedicate themselves to each other, coming together to form a union sexually, emotionally, intellectually, financially, and so on. They remain distinct individuals, but they commit themselves to one another. In other words, marriage is an other-centered, not self-centered, relationship.

Marriage is also to be monogamous and two-gendered: one woman for one man. No same-sex, bigamist, or polygamist relationships allowed.

When Adam and the Woman married, they "felt no shame" even though they were naked (Genesis 2:25). In other words, they were transparent to each other, accepting of each other, and intimate with each other. Nothing, internal or external, concealed them from each other. The revelation between them was full and free. "Indeed, basking in the sunshine of all their blessings, the man and woman in their nakedness enjoyed the glorious liberty of the children of God."[47]

• *What do you think about the biblical description of marriage? Do you agree or disagree with it? Do you find it restrictive or liberating? Explain your answer.*

A Great Start

What an amazing start! A good and beautiful world. Creatures flying in the sky. A growing abundance of plant and animal life. All kinds of water creatures reproducing in oceans, seas, and rivers. And in the midst of it all, Eden—a garden paradise created specifically for the first human couple to love, play, work, and commune with each other and with the One who created it all—the triune God. All was good and right with the world.

Tragically, it does not last. And the consequences that follow from that loss are the focus of the rest of Scripture and the lives of every human being that has come into this world ever since.

Talking It Out

1. Genesis 2 conveys the beauty, goodness, and nourishment of Eden, as well as the wonderful creation and intimacy of the first human couple. What about that picture

resonates with your longings—perhaps for more beauty, harmony, transparency, joy, or flourishing—in your life and relationships? Do you think any of those longings can be met, even partially, in this world? Explain your answer.

2. Now imagine you are one of the members of the first human couple. You are in Eden, a plush and beautiful utopia. You are enjoying life with your mate, nature, and God. What might a typical day be like? Or would any day be typical? Do your best to picture yourself and describe what you would do, how you would feel, and what you would want to talk about with your spouse and with God.

3. The Bible opens with a utopia and closes with one. Read Revelation 21:1–22:5. What similarities and differences do you find between the new world of the opening chapters of Genesis and the renewed world of Revelation? What does this tell you about where history is headed?

LESSON 6

The Tempter and the Temptation

(3:1-6)

We're not told how much time elapsed between the first couple's creation in innocence and their disobedience against God. The first two chapters of Genesis, however, make it clear that the first man and woman lived in a wonderful environment in which all their needs were met and their communion with each other and with God was unbroken. They knew who and what they were, they were betrothed by God, they were transparent to each other and to God, and they were divinely led and instructed. All was good and well.

The Tempter

- *Who makes his appearance in Genesis 3:1? Consult TPT study note 'f' for verse 1 to learn more about the tempter. Jot down what you find that helps you identify who this was.*

• *Who made "the snake" according to verse 1?*

• *Was this creature originally good? To answer this question, consult the verses from Genesis 1 that follow and jot down what you find about God's initial creation.*

Verse 10

Verse 12

Verse 18

Verse 25

Verse 27

Verse 31

- *Given what you found, circle the words below that best describe God's original handiwork:*

  Good or evil

  Beautiful or ugly

  Uncorrupted or corrupted

  Ordered or disordered

  Teeming with life or marred by disease and death

The biblical evidence supports the conclusion that "the snake" that shows up in Genesis 3 was one of God's creatures that he created to be good but that revolted against him and became morally evil. Later revelation identifies this creature as Satan, the devil, an originally good angelic being who rebelled against the Creator.

- *To learn more about him, read through the following passages and write down what they say about him:*

  John 8:44

2 Corinthians 11:3, 14

1 John 3:8

Revelation 12:3–4, 7–9

Genesis does not record when the rebellion of this angel occurred. All Genesis relates to us is that God's original creation was completely good before evil entered it. Satan suddenly comes on the scene at the start of chapter 3, and his words and actions show that he is against God and his image bearers.

THE EXTRA MILE

Although Genesis does not speak to how a good angel turned bad, other Bible books may. Two are Isaiah (14:12–14) and Ezekiel (28:12–19).

The Isaiah passage is sandwiched inside a prophecy of divine judgment that will come against one of Israel's enemies, Babylon (Isaiah 13:1–14:23).[48] Many scholars see 14:12–14 as a description of Satan's initial rebellion. The church fathers Tertullian (ca. CE 160–230) and Gregory the Great (ca. 540–604) were the first to present this view. This became the widely accepted interpretation, but two others have been offered. One is that these verses are only describing the Babylonian king's sin of pride, using hyperbolic language to capture it (e.g., terms such as "I will ascend into heaven," "exalt my throne above the stars of God," "I will rise past the tops of the clouds and rival the Most High God"). Another view is that the prophet Isaiah is describing the sin of the earthly king as well as that of the demonic power behind him.

For many of today's Bible scholars, the textual evidence is stronger that Satan is the focus in Ezekiel 28:12–19 than in the Isaiah verses. In Ezekiel, the passages occur in a much larger judgment prophecy against Tyre (26:1–28:19). Chapters 26 and 27 are aimed at the city-state of Tyre. Chapter 28 opens up with judgments against the human leader or ruler of that once great city (28:1–10) while the judgments recorded in verses 11 through 19 are directed against "the king of Tyre" (v. 12). The descriptions of this king seem beyond hyperbole and simply don't fit a human being. In his book *Angels: Elect and Evil*, C. Fred Dickason points out some of the key differences between the ruler/leader addressed in verses 1 through 10 and the king judged in verses 12 through 19:

> [Differences include] (1) different titles, "prince" (leader) and "king"; (2) different natures, "man" (vv. 2, 9), and "the anointed cherub" (v. 14), "O covering cherub" (v. 16); the superlatives used of the king, "full of wisdom and perfect in beauty" (v. 12); (4) the perfection of the king, "You were blameless in your ways from the day you were created" (v. 15, NASB). For these reasons we take Ezekiel 28:12–19 to refer to Satan.[49]

In his commentary on Ezekiel, Charles H. Dyer adds more reasons that support the view that Satan is the primary subject of Ezekiel 28:12–19:

> In 28:1–10 Ezekiel rebuked the *ruler* for claiming to be a god though he was just a

man. But in verses 11–19 Ezekiel described the *king* in terms that could not apply to a mere man. This "king" had appeared in the Garden of Eden (v. 13), had been a guardian cherub (v. 14a), had possessed free access to God's holy mountain (v. 14b), and had been sinless from the time he was created (v. 15)...

Ezekiel was not describing an ideal man or false god in verses 11–26. But his switch from "ruler" to "king" and his allusions to the Garden of Eden do imply that the individual being described was more than human. The best explanation is that Ezekiel was describing Satan who was the true "king" of Tyre, the one motivating the human "ruler" of Tyre. Satan was in the Garden of Eden (Gen. 3:1–7), and his chief sin was pride (1 Tim. 3:6). He also had access to God's presence (cf. Job 1:6–12). Speaking of God's judging the human "ruler" of Tyre for his pride (Ezek. 28:1–10), the prophet lamented the satanic "king" of Tyre who was also judged for his pride (vv. 11–19). Tyre was motivated by the same sin as Satan, and would suffer the same fate.[50]

- *Assuming that Ezekiel 28:11–19 refers to Satan, the power supporting the human ruler's charge over Tyre, write below what you learn about Satan as you read through those verses.*

- *Turning back to Isaiah 14:12–14 and assuming that they provide insight into Satan's initial rebellion against God, note below what they reveal about this sinful event.*

The Temptation

Satan approached the woman and deceptively challenged God's word, veracity, and motive.

- *What did Satan first say to the woman (Genesis 3:1)? How does his question differ from what God had actually told Adam in 2:16–17?*

- *What was the woman's response to Satan's question (3:2–3)? What did she add to God's original command (cf. 2:17)?*

- *What was Satan's response to the woman (3:4–5)? What did he say that directly contradicted God's command? How did he challenge God's motives?*

- *How would you sum up Satan's caricature of God? From his comments, what would you say that Satan tried to get the woman to believe about her Creator?*

- *Did Satan's temptation of the woman work (3:6)? What was the woman's response, and why did she make it?*

- *How did Adam respond to what his wife did?*

⚘ EXPERIENCE GOD'S HEART

- *What temptations do you struggle with the most? Why do you find them so alluring?*

- *When you give in to temptation, what is the remedy (1 John 1:8–10)?*

- *We can also resist temptation, including Satan's attempts to draw us away from God. Read James 4:1–10. What do these verses reveal about how we can withstand temptation as we strive to stay aligned with the Lord?*

♥ SHARE GOD'S HEART

In Ephesians 6:10–18, the apostle Paul counsels the believers in Ephesus about how they can successfully battle Satan's attacks. While we can certainly apply Paul's instructions to our individual lives, his battle strategy is primarily for groups of believers to incorporate into their life together.

- *What does Paul say about our common enemy?*

- *What are the pieces of armor, weapons, and actions we should make part of our lives, and how will they affect our fight against the devil?*

- *What part of Paul's counsel do you lack most or find to be your greatest challenge? Why? What can you start doing to overcome this weakness in your spiritual battle with the evil one? Your self-preparation is an important way to contribute to fighting the battles faced by the groups of believers to which you belong.*

ⓖ DIGGING DEEPER

The writer of Genesis doesn't tell us what Adam was doing during the temptation of his wife. All he says is that Adam was "with her" (3:6) before he joined in her disobedience to God. But we do know that God's original command about what to eat and not eat in the garden was given to Adam before the woman was even created. We have no record that God gave the same command to the woman, and yet she knew it and even added words to it. The implication is that Adam passed along God's command to his wife. If this is so, then Adam knew God's command firsthand, and the woman knew it secondhand. As to who first added words to the command, we don't know with certainty. Adam may have done so when he told his wife about the forbidden tree. Or the woman may have added those words to reinforce her own resolve to keep away from the tree. Either way, the addition didn't keep her or Adam from disobeying their Creator.

Moreover, although Paul emphasizes in 1 Timothy that "Adam did not mislead Eve, but Eve misled him and violated the command of God" (2:14), the apostle places the onus of responsibility on Adam, not Eve, when it comes to treating humanity's initial sin and the consequences that flowed from that (Romans 5:12–21). Perhaps that's because God *directly* commanded Adam to abstain from eating from the forbidden tree. Adam knew firsthand, and he had spent even more time with God before Eve was ever made. He could have also tried to prevent Eve from falling for Satan's temptation, and he certainly could have chosen not to follow her in sin. He could have also served as an advocate before God for his disobedient wife. But Adam did none of these things. For these reasons at least, he bears the greater weight of responsibility for humanity's fall from innocence.

Talking It Out

1. Bible scholars often relate Genesis 3 to 1 John 2:16–17 when they comment on the first temptation and sin and the pattern of rebellion they established: "For all that the world can offer us—the gratification of our flesh, the allurement of the things of the world, and the obsession with status and importance—none of these things come from the Father but from the world. This world and its desires are in the process of passing away, but those who love to do the will of God will live forever." Compare what the apostle John says here with what lured Adam and Eve to rebel against God. What similarities do you see? In what ways do the temptations of the world pull you away from your Creator, Sustainer, and Savior?

2. The tempter's tactic in Genesis 3 was to twist and undermine God's words and to call into question God's motives. When Satan tempted Jesus in the wilderness of Palestine, what were his tactics, and how did they compare to what he did in Eden (Luke 4:1–13)? What insights does this comparison give for what we can expect from Satan today? And what does Jesus' response to Satan's temptations reveal about how we can effectively combat the most deadly and dangerous enemy of our faith?

3. Adam followed his wife in revolt against God. Discuss the influence others often have in our relationship with God. What are some positive ways people can help us to stay aligned with God? What are some negative ways people use to draw us away from our allegiance to God? What steps can we take to take advantage of the positive influences while refusing the negative ones?

LESSON 7

Revolt, Loss, and Promise

(3:7–24)

When God gave Adam the command not to eat from the Tree that gives the knowledge of good and evil, he said that the transgression would bring certain death (Genesis 2:17). The Hebrew literally reads, "dying you will die." In his commentary on the first chapters of Genesis, Henri Blocher provides insight into a biblical view of death, especially as presented in Genesis 2 and 3:

> In the Bible, death is the reverse of life—it is not the reverse of existence. To die does not mean to cease to be, but in biblical terms it means 'cut off from the land of the living', henceforth unable to act, and to enter another condition. Even in the Old Testament, when the revelation of the life beyond is shrouded in mist, and despite the affinity between death and destruction, since death disintegrates the power to live, this condition is not confused with the extinction of being. It is diminished existence, but nevertheless an existence. Proof of this is found in the representation of the departed as meeting in 'the house appointed for all living' (Jb. 30:23), who are

'joined to their fathers' and who greet and speak to one another (Is. 14; Ezk. 32)...

This is important for Genesis...[S]ince dying is still existing, other changes in existence will, by extension, be able to bear the name of 'death'. In all the experiences of pain, discomfort, discord and separation, we can recognize a kind of funeral procession...This is the precise viewpoint of Genesis 3. The narrative shows us that the threat 'You shall die' is fulfilled in a multiplicity of ways, by a whole succession of disastrous changes.[51]

In Scripture, death involves separation from the eternal and living God, the One who is the very source of all life. And that separation affects everything else that humanity experiences: his relationship with himself and others; his work and play; his bodily and spiritual life; his interaction with the natural world...nothing is untouched, nothing left uncorrupted. Nothing is as it should be or could have been. Death marks everything.[52]

While the first man and first woman did not experience physical death immediately, they experienced death in other ways right away.

- *Read Genesis 3:7–13 and answer the following questions:*

  What changed in the couple's relationship as husband and wife and as individuals?

What changed in the couple's relationship to the garden? Were they still enjoying it, or were they using it in unintended ways? Explain your answer.

What changed in their relationship to God?

What changed in their relationship to the snake?

Would you say that the first couple was better off or worse off after they disobeyed God? What was the most significant change that supports your answer?

Following God's confrontation with Adam and the woman in which he gave each one the opportunity to confess their wrongdoing, the Lord turned to his role as judge.

A Curse and a Promise

Despite what Adam and the woman did, God did not curse them. Instead he cursed the shining snake, the serpent, Satan himself.

- *What was the divine curse pronounced on the snake, the symbol of Satan (v. 14)?*

Blocher points out that the Hebrew prophets "show that in the snake eating the dust they saw the humiliation of pagan power and the overthrow of the forces of evil (Is. 65:25; Mi. 7:17). Genesis in point of fact is making use of the snake symbolism; its crawling, which classifies it amongst abominable beasts (Lv. 11:42), acts as a symbol for the humiliation of that spirit of opposition to God represented by the snake."[53]

Along with the curse, God gave a promise that would unfold in human history.

- *What did God promise to his Adversary (Genesis 3:15)? Read the two study notes on this verse to gain added insight for your answer.*

- *The following passages add more light to the promise made in Genesis 3:15. Look up each reference and jot down what you find that relates to the war between Satan and the woman's descendants, especially those who are now "in Christ":*

Zechariah 3:1–2

Romans 16:19–20

Hebrews 2:14–18

1 Peter 5:8

Revelation 12

The Woman's Sentence

- *What was the divine judge's sentence upon the woman as a result of her disobedience (Genesis 3:16)? Consider the study notes on this passage as well and then record your observations and reflections.*

The Man's Sentence

- *God judged the tempter first and then the first one to fall prey to the tempter. Finally, he turned to Adam, the first human being God had made, befriended, and blessed. What was his judgment on Adam (vv. 17–19)? Also read through the study notes on these verses to add important information to your observations and reflections on these verses.*

A Name Change

- *Although death entered the human realm through human sin, Adam still saw in his wife the gift of life. This is reflected in the name he gave her (v. 20). What was that name, and what does the name mean? For help, see the study note on this verse.*

Merciful Redemption and Banishment

With judgment pronounced, God provided redemption. He had already promised the eventual defeat of Satan in 3:15, a promise that would reach its fulfillment in the Messiah, Jesus, and his conquering and saving death on Golgotha's cross. But in verse 21, God shed the blood of animals he had created and from them made clothing for Adam and Eve. In doing so, God covered the first couple's nakedness, over which they were now ashamed, and he showed them that the cost of sin and salvation must be the shedding of blood in sacrifice. God clothed them with much more than rags or loincloths. As Brian Simmons says, "This verb ('to clothe') is mostly used for kings who clothe others with robes (see Gen. 41:42), or for priests who are clothed with sacred garments (see Ex. 28:41; 29:8; 40:14)."[54] Adam and Eve were still God's rulers and stewards of his creation, so he clothed them appropriately. Their sin didn't take away from them the divine commission they had received (Genesis 1:28–30). But it would lead to their expulsion from Eden.

• *Read Genesis 3:22–24 and the study notes on these verses. Record below what you find.*

Banished from Eden and the Tree of Life, Adam and Eve were left to make their way in a world now cursed and marked by death and corruption. But in barring them from the Tree of Life, God also showed his mercy. Imagine living forever in a sinful condition, living a life of ongoing diminishment, a life that would always be frustrated, marked by trouble, anguish, despair, alienation, and so many other kinds of suffering. This would be an awful existence, a hell on earth. God kept them from that end by denying them access to the Tree of Life. From this point forward, humanity's home would not be found on earth nor would his search for meaning and the fullness of life. He would have to look to heaven, to the One he should have relied on before the first sin: the Lord, the Giver of life, the Creator of all that's good, the only One who can save from sin, Satan, and death.

Also, by expelling Adam and Eve from Eden and the Tree of Life, God was exposing what had really happened to them when they followed Satan's deception. Satan claimed that they would become "like God, knowing both good and evil" (3:5). They would become their own gods, living independently of God, judging what is wise without reference to him but only in relation to themselves. Is this what they actually received from their sin? Did they now know wisdom as God does?

Not at all! God is the source of all wisdom (Proverbs 2:6; 3:19; Jeremiah 10:12), truth (John 1:14; 14:6; 17:17; Titus 1:2), and goodness (Exodus 34:6–7; 2 Chronicles 7:3; Psalm 36:5–9; 136; Acts 14:16–17), and he is all-knowing (Psalm 139:1–6; 147:4–5;

Isaiah 40:12–14, 26–28; Romans 11:33–34). Adam and Eve gained none of this. What they did gain was the experience of something they had not experienced before—evil. They had knowledge of what God had forbidden and what the consequence would be, but they had no firsthand experience of evil and its fruit. In choosing disobedience over obedience, they acted foolishly, yielded to deception, and committed evil. They then learned things they had not known before. But would anyone say that they were now better off, that they were now wiser than they were before? Satan's promise was an illusion. What Adam and Eve inherited was the fruit of foolishness, not of wisdom, and the fruit that brought death, not immortal life.

Adam and Eve did gain a measure of independence from God—an independence that left them expelled from paradise, barred from the Tree of Life, and with a life marked by death, a lost innocence, and estrangement from God, one another, their individual selves, and their natural surroundings. Their gain was filled with great losses.

 EXPERIENCE GOD'S HEART

- *Have you ever strived to achieve a goal that you thought would bring gain to your life only to find that what you gained was outmeasured by what you lost? Describe that situation and what you learned through it.*

- *No matter what roads we travel that lead to dead ends,*
  God is there to redeem and restore us to himself though
  we may still have to endure some of the consequences.
  Take time now to show your gratitude to him for sticking
  with you and not abandoning you, for graciously and
  mercifully forgiving you and working to restore you.

♥ SHARE GOD'S HEART

We live in a day and time where few people acknowledge or accept the reality of human rebellion against God and his Word. But we cannot move forward with him until we grasp the truth about our human condition. Genesis 3 leaves no doubt how sin entered humanity's line. As the rest of Genesis unfolds, we'll see how sin spreads and how much damage it does.

- *Knowing that humanity has been deceived and even*
  intentionally continues going astray, how should this
  influence the way you see and relate to unbelieving
  neighbors—family members, friends, work associates,
  church attendees, and the like? Note how God responded
  to the sin of Adam and Eve; he demonstrated a heavenly

application of wisdom that involved the recognition of their sin and the remedy for it. He treated them as his image bearers all the way through, from their innocence through their wrongdoing and guilt. How can you treat others in ways that still acknowledge them as image bearers but image bearers who have gone wrong and need salvation?

Talking It Out

1. Adam didn't help his wife avoid sin, and after he rebelled against God with her, he blamed her for what he had done. Have you joined with others in their wrongdoing? When you have been caught doing wrong, have you shifted the blame away from yourself? How did you feel after you did such things? What can you do to right such wrongs? What can you do to restore your relationship with God? You may want to consult 1 John 1:5–10.

2. What are some losses you have endured as consequences
   of your sin? What did you learn through those losses? Have
   you used these lessons to help others? If so, how?

3. Human life began in a God-designed utopia (Genesis 2).
   For those individuals whose names are found in the Book
   of Life, a new God-designed utopia will be theirs to live in
   forever (Revelation 20:11–22:5). Do you think human beings
   can create a utopia? Why or why not?

LESSON 8

Life, Family, and Fracture

(4:1–5:32)

Have you ever reflected on some of this world's instances of mayhem, violence, abuse, suffering, and pain and remarked to yourself, "Things are not as they should be"? That instinct and assessment of life in this world is exactly right. The corruption and destruction, despair and hurt, and even natural catastrophes are not what God wanted for us. He designed us for a utopian existence: a life of incredible beauty, abiding goodness, foundational order, freedom to love, marry, raise families, do meaningful work, be creative, rest, play...to do all these things and more and all in growing communion with him. God made us to be image bearers living every day in joy and peace with one another and with the One who made them.

Human rebellion changed all of this. When Adam and Eve turned away from God and turned toward themselves, pitting their wills against his, they brought death into life, evil into goodness, ugliness into beauty, disorder into order, and slavery into freedom. The world changed. Utopia came to an end. What was and should have remained were lost—but not forevermore.

God had a plan of redemption. A way to overcome what humanity forfeited.

So as sin's consequences grew, God's grace grew more. The rest of Genesis shows how these realities started to shape human life and history.

The First Family

The latter part of Book 1 in Genesis (chapter 4) reveals that the first married couple obeyed God's directive to "reproduce and be fruitful" (Genesis 1:28).

- *Who were the first fruits of Adam and Eve's reproductive relations (4:1–2)? What was their gender, and which one of them was born first?*

- *From whom did the first woman come (2:22)? From whom did the first male child come?*

- *Now read Paul's reflection on these events in 1 Corinthians 11:7–12. From what Paul says, what should the relationship between men and women be?*

- *Do you think Paul has reasoned well from what Genesis presents about the interdependency of men and women? Are there any other lines of reasoning and evidence you might bring to bear on this biblical picture of male and female? If so, what are they?*

- *Returning to Genesis 4:2, what was Cain's vocational choice? What was Abel's?*

Sacrifice and Murder

After introducing the two sons, the writer turns to an event that involved making a sacrifice to Yahweh. No doubt Adam and Eve had raised their sons with stories about life in Eden, including what led to their exile from that garden. The sons must have heard how God had killed some animals and formed clothing from their skins to cover their parents' nakedness and to show how redemption requires a blood sacrifice. We can easily imagine that Adam and Eve carried on that practice of sacrifice in their relationship before God, probably involving their children in that form of worship.

Now on their own, Cain and Abel carry out their lives, with Cain working the land to raise crops and Abel raising and caring for animals. On one of the occasions where they prepare to worship, each man brings something different to offer to God.

- *What did Cain offer to God (Genesis 4:3)? Are there any descriptions of Cain's offering that would give you the impression that he brought to sacrifice the best of what he had to offer?*

- *What was God's response to Cain's offering (v. 5)?*

- *Now consider Abel's offering (v. 4). What did he bring, and how did God regard it? What about Abel's offering was different from Cain's? See study note 'e' on verse 3 for additional information about the two offerings from the two sons.*

- *Cain found God's response to him unacceptable. What does the text say that Cain felt (v. 5)?*

- *Consider God's response to Cain (vv. 6–7). What does he say about Cain's offering that further indicates what was wrong with it? What warning did he give Cain?*

🅝 WORD WEALTH

According to Old Testament scholar Bruce Waltke, the word translated "offering" in verse 3 is *minha*, "the common Hebrew word for 'tribute'…With this offering, the giver acknowledges the superiority or rule of the receiver (Lev. 2:14; 1 Sam. 10:27; 1 Kings 10:25). Both Cain and Abel bring an offering. They both come as priests, worship the same God, and desire God's acceptance, but only Abel brings acceptable tribute."[55]

What made Abel's offering acceptable and Cain's unacceptable? The writer doesn't mention any difference between the offerings except one of quality. Abel's came from "the finest of the firstborn of his flocks" (Genesis 4:4). Nothing to indicate the quality of the offering comes from the writer's description of what Cain brought.

Moreover, Cain displayed a "heart and character [that] were not right with God."[56] This came out in his rage against the Lord and later in the terrible action he took against his own brother.

• *Knowing what God thought of his offering, imagine some responses Cain could have made that would have been good and responsible. Record your thoughts here.*

• *Now write down how Cain actually responded (v. 8).*

 WORD WEALTH

The Hebrew word translated "killed" in verse 8 "is used particularly of ruthless violence by private persons."[57] Commenting on Cain's actions, Waltke says: "Cain's bad feelings against God spill over into irrational behavior and an unjustifiable jealous rage against his brother. The sundering of the familial bond, begun in [Genesis] chapter 3, here escalates to fratricide in one mere generation."[58]

- *After Cain murders Abel, an exchange occurs between Yahweh and Cain (4:9–15). Summarize the dialogue.*

- *What did Yahweh do to quell Cain's fear that what he did to his own brother might be done to him (v. 15)?*

- *What did Cain do following his exchange with Yahweh (v. 16)?*

- *Compare the following passages from Genesis. Jot down the similarities and dissimilarities you find. What do you think may be their significance in revealing the deepening corruption of humanity and God's response to it?*

Compare 3:9 with 4:9

Compare 3:12–13 with 4:5

Compare 3:17 with 4:11–12

Compare 3:21 with 4:15

Compare 3:23–24 with 4:16

The Line of Cain

Most of the rest of Genesis 4 gives us the line of Cain—a genealogy never expanded on in the rest of Scripture.

- *Write down the names of those among Cain's descendants who did more than simply procreate. What did those individuals do, for good or ill (4:17–22)?*

Sinfulness doesn't bar creativeness or inventiveness as Cain's line shows. Construction, metallurgy, and music began with his descendants—descendants who also came from Adam and Eve. Image bearers displayed different applications of the abilities first granted to them by their Creator. At the same time, Cain's line shows no Godward inclination, nothing indicating that they looked to Yahweh, worshiped or served Yahweh, or credited him for their blessings. Civilization without God. Culture and creativity without the Creator. The One who enabled them to live, work, reproduce, invent, and do all other good things went unacknowledged and unappreciated. Many thousands of years later, the apostle Paul reflected on human history and said, "Throughout human history the fingerprints of God were upon them, yet they refused to honor him as God or even be thankful for his kindness" (Romans 1:21).

When the Life-Giver is set aside, the value of human life diminishes; it can even become cheap. Lamech, one of Cain's descendants, was the first recorded bigamist (Genesis 4:19), showing that he did not care about God's original design for marriage (2:24). He also took murder to a new and worse level.

- *Using poetry as his communication medium, Lamech boasts to his wives about what he did. Read Genesis 4:23–24 and summarize below what Lamech said he did and what he thought he deserved as a result.*

The first recorded poem celebrated the wonder of Eve's creation and Adam's devotion to her (2:23). Lamech's poem celebrates his murder of another human being for a personal offense. The first poem praises God's achievement; the second praises oneself for achieving vengeance through violence. The first poem praises a creative act; the second poem boasts about a destructive act.

Furthermore, Cain's initial attempt to avoid responsibility for the death of Abel (4:9) escalates to Lamech showing pride over the murder he's committed (v. 23). The descendants of inventors have also invented violence within civilization. Sin birthed brutality. The wisdom Adam and Eve sought when they took from the forbidden tree led at least some of their descendants to deception, irrational justifications, murder, and even the celebration of human depravity while surrounded by the inventiveness and life-bearing abilities God's image bearers had. The history of us was well on its way.

The Line of Seth

God had promised in Genesis 3:15 that from Eve's seed would come One who would win the war against Satan. That while Satan's seed would engage in hostilities against Eve's seed, eventually her seed would crush Satan's head, delivering the fatal blow. Cain's line represents Satan's seed. Its increasing fall into depravity's depths displayed Satan's side, not God's. Fortunately, Cain's line, as God promised, would not have the last word.

Beginning in 4:25, the writer moves away from Cain's descendants, returns to Adam and Eve, and presents the line of descendants who came after Abel and at least generally followed after his heart for God.

- *For Adam's and Eve's descendants through Seth (4:25–5:32), create a diagram that shows who fathered whom. Under each name, record any details about the person's life or family and how long each person lived.*

- *This is the first time in Scripture that the length of one's life is recorded. Look back over the number of years that each person lived. What do you notice?*

- *Why do you think the writer has highlighted the time length of so many people's lives? Consider Genesis 2:17 and 3:19 in your answer.*

- *What in 4:25–5:32 indicates to you that at least some of the descendants in Seth's line looked to God and served him?*

- *Enoch is one of Seth's descendants who stands out in the genealogical list. Consult 5:21–24 and study note 'a' for verses 23–24. Jot down what you discover about this man of God.*

Seth's genealogy in Genesis 5 (which begins with the second *toledot* section, Book 2) ends with Noah and his three sons (vv. 28–32). It will be through Noah and his family that humanity will be saved through divine judgment on human wickedness run amok. It will also be through Seth that the conquering seed of Eve will eventually come (Luke 3:28).

- *Cain's line gives a glimpse into life lived apart from God, while Seth's line starts to reveal what life can be when God is at the center of it. With whose line do you identify and why?*

 DIGGING DEEPER

A common question that arises when it comes to the genealogies of Seth and Cain and the mention of marriages and children is: Who did Adam and Eve's descendants marry in order for them to fulfill God's command to "reproduce and be fruitful" and "populate the earth" (Genesis 1:28)? The answer is, family members married other family members. Old Testament scholar Gleason Archer puts the matter this way:

> Genesis 5:4 tells us that during Adam's long lifetime of 930 years (800 after the birth of Seth), he had other sons and daughters. Since he and Eve had been ordered to produce a large family in order to populate the earth (Gen. 1:28), it is reasonable to assume that they continued to have children for a long period of time, under the then ideal conditions for longevity.
>
> Without question it was necessary for the generation following Adam to pair off brothers and sisters to serve as parents for the ensuing generation; otherwise the human race would have died off. It was not until the course of subsequent generations that it became possible for cousins and more distant relations to choose each other as marriage partners. There seems to be no definite word about the incestuous character of brother-sister marriage until the time of Abraham, who emphasized to the Egyptians that Sarah was his sister (cf. Gen. 20:12), thus implying to the Egyptians that if she was his sister, she could not be his wife (Gen. 12:13).
>
> In Leviticus 20:17 the actual sanction against brother-sister marriage is spelled out. But as for Cain and Seth and all the other sons of Adam who married, they must have chosen their sisters as wives.[59]

❤ EXPERIENCE GOD'S HEART

Family is God's idea, his plan for us. And so is the means for having family—sexual relations, reproduction. Family and sex can be abused in a fallen world, just as marriage or any other good thing can. But that doesn't take away from their inherent goodness. Take away the evil that occurs in a marriage or family and what do you have but a much better marriage and family. Evil diminishes and destroys. It is like rust in metal; evil eats away at what is meant to be good. But remove the evil—the rust—and what you have is better, the good.

In Adam and Eve's line of descendants, we begin to see what can happen when God is at the center of marriage and family life and when he is not. Seth's line shows the former while Cain's line shows the latter. The more Genesis unfolds, the more details it reveals about godly and ungodly living and their different consequences. For now, let's turn our attention to some of what we can glean about our marriages and families in light of human life after the first couple's initial rebellion.

- *What was your family life like growing up? Was it more good than evil or more evil than good?*

- *How has your family life influenced your self-image? Do you see yourself as a divine image bearer or something less?*

- *If you are married, is it a relationship in which you are honored and encouraged to flourish? If so, what does that look like in your marriage? If not, what does that look like?*

- *If you are unmarried, what is your view of marriage? Is this a relationship you want for your life? Why or why not?*

- *Now consider your maleness or femaleness. How are you treated in light of your gender? Explain your answer.*

- *Do you see sex as God does—as a good and beautiful act designed for marriage (Genesis 2:24; Hebrews 13:4)? Why or why not?*

- *If you find yourself out of sync with God's view of marriage, family, and sex, what might you do to help you bring your life into line with his teaching and thereby enjoy the good fruit of that realignment?*

 SHARE GOD'S HEART

- *How has your family life influenced your relationships with fellow human beings and with God?*

- *God designed marriage and family to be good things in our lives, to help us flourish, including in our walk with him. If you are married and/or have children, how are you contributing to your spouse and/or children so they can become better rather than worse, so their knowledge, wisdom, character, and walk with God can grow in truth, goodness, and beauty?*

Talking It Out

1. Compare human life as presented in Genesis 1–2 with human life as depicted in chapters 4 and 5. Talk about how you think life would have developed if no sin had entered the picture. Would some of what's mentioned in Genesis 4–5 have become part of a sin-free world? Support your answer.

2. Marriage and family life fractured from Genesis 3 on. What do you see today as further signs of that fracturing? What would at least be a start to healing those relationships or perhaps developing better ones?

3. Abel's appearance in Genesis is brief, but he is not forgotten. Look up the following passages and jot down what they reveal about Abel: Matthew 23:34–35; Hebrews 11:4; 1 John 3:11–12. Given what these texts say, is there anything you would add about Abel and his actions that you didn't glean from Genesis 4? Also, did you find anything about Cain and his killing of Abel that added to your understanding of Cain and his sin?

LESSON 9

Noah and the Judgment to Come

(6:1–22)

Any good created thing can become corrupted.

- Eyes designed to see can grow dim and even blind or can be used in lustful ways.

- Ears designed to hear can gradually lose their ability and become deaf or can be used to soak in gossip and graphic music.

- Marriages meant to last for life can fracture through betrayal, abuse, desertion, and even disinterest before coming to an end.

- Worthwhile and achievable dreams can dwindle away and even be crushed or can be sought after for selfish gain instead of God's glory.

- Thriving and fulfilling vocations can be undermined and even terminated through economic downturns, slander, bigotry, severe errors in judgment, and a host of other factors.

- Families meant for mutual support and growth can become distant, adversarial, and cruel.

The only incorruptible good is God (Psalm 100:5; James 1:13–14; 1 John 1:5). Everything—and everyone—else can turn bad, go wrong, fail to achieve what it was designed to do.

Adam and Eve were designed to image God in all they said and did, in their character and relationships, in their work and play, in their worship and service. But they chose evil over good, the illusion of wisdom over genuine wisdom, death over life. This did irreparable damage to their humanity. Every new human life from conception to death would bear this damage.

While still good in what we are—human beings who bear the image of God—we also show the signs of corruption.[60] We are image bearers who will sin and die. We will hurt others as well as ourselves. We will suffer diseases, shame, guilt, broken relationships, dashed dreams, and many other signs of brokenness. All of us are damaged goods.

Genesis 6 continues the story of the corruption of God's good and beautiful creation. What we'll see as the story unfolds is what God did to counter the evil rippling through what he had made. His judgment was severe, but it also came with hope and salvation. Humanity was not abandoned. That is not the way of him who is loving, merciful, and gracious.

Human Wickedness

An Unholy Union

- *Genesis 6:1–2 and 4 (the continuation of Book 2) describe one of the strangest incidents in biblical history. Read these verses and summarize what they say without consulting the study notes.*

- *From what these verses say, what would you conclude are the "divine beings" (v. 2) and "heavenly beings" (v. 4)?*

⏻ DIGGING DEEPER

The Hebrew words translated "divine beings" and "heavenly beings" can be literally rendered "the sons of the gods" or "the sons of God."[61] This phrase can refer to angels or spirits (Job 1:6; 2:1; Psalm 29:1; 89:6) or to human beings (Deuteronomy 14:1; Psalm 73:15; Hosea 1:10). This is one key reason why Bible scholars have interpreted the Genesis 6 uses of this phrase differently. The interpretations vary over the nature of these "sons." What were they?

One interpretation sees the "sons of the gods/God" as human beings who were from the godly line of Seth. On this view, the descendants of Seth were enticed by the ungodly women of Cain's line and so "took the women they wanted as their wives" (Genesis 6:2).[62] A problem with this interpretation is that Genesis never refers to the entire line of Seth as godly (though some members of the line were godly, and through Seth's line the Messiah would eventually come).[63] Another problem is that the women or daughters "in this context refers to Seth's [line], for in his lineage the begetting of daughters is repeated nine times (5:4, 7, passim), and the narrator never mentions daughters in Cain's lineage."[64]

Another interpretation is that the "sons of the gods/God" refers to "royal tyrannical successors of Lamech." This is based on "an ancient Jewish interpretation that the 'sons of God' were nobles, aristocrats, and princes who married girls outside their social status and took great numbers of them into their harems." These tyrants from Lamech's line "were supposed to administer justice, but instead they claimed for themselves deity, violated the divine order by forming royal harems, and perverted their mandate to rule the earth under God."[65] So the "sons" of Genesis 6 were human kings who claimed to be gods. While this interpretation better fits the context of Genesis 6, it conflicts with certain understandings of 2 Peter 2:4–5 and Jude 6–7 that see these passages as New Testament commentary on Genesis 6:2—a commentary that views the "sons" as sinful, demonic angels.

This takes us to a third interpretation of Genesis 6:2, which views the "sons of the gods/God" as fallen angels. As the study note on this passage says, "Virtually all of the earliest writings of Jewish and Christian literature interpret the phrase 'the sons of the gods' as heavenly beings known as fallen angels or 'watchers.'"[66] In other words, these were corrupt angelic beings who married human women, had intercourse with them, and produced offspring that came to be known as "the mighty ones of old, warriors of renown" (v. 4). Criticisms of this interpretation are mostly based on the nature of angels. Angels are spirit beings, and Jesus said that "a spirit does not have a body of flesh and bone" (Luke 24:39); in other words, spirits have no physical bodies and so cannot have physical relations with human beings. Moreover, Jesus also said that angels do not marry nor are given in marriage (Matthew 22:30). Therefore, it seems that angelic beings, even sinful ones, did not marry and produce offspring with human women. Gleason Archer raises one other problem with this interpretive option that sees "the sons of the gods/God" as fallen angels—demons:

> If they were minions of Satan, that is,
> fallen angels, then they could not have
> been referred to as "sons of God." Demons
> of hell would never be so designated in
> Scripture. Nor could they have been angels
> of God, since God's angels always live in
> total obedience to Him and have no other

yearning or desire but to do God's will and glorify His name. A sordid involvement with godless young women would therefore be completely out of character for angels as "sons of God."[67]

Because of the problems of each of the above views, some commentators propose that "the sons of the gods/God" in Genesis 6:2 were human beings who became demon possessed, and the demonic spirits influencing them led them "to interbreed with 'the daughters of men,' [which produced] a superior breed whose offspring were the 'giants' and 'men of renown [of v. 4]'"[68] So demon spirit beings used corrupt human rulers as intermediaries to marry and have sexual relations with women. This interpretation appears to combine the best of the other views while avoiding their problems.

- *Did any of these interpretive choices alter your initial understanding of the opening verses of Genesis 6? If so, in what ways? If not, why?*

The Divine Declaration

God never sits back and just watches what goes on in his creation. He's always engaged with it. And this early part of human history was no exception.

- *Genesis 6:5, 11, and 12 reveal God's assessment of human behavior. What was it? How bad had the human race become?*

- *How did God feel toward humanity at this time in history? Read verse 6 and study note 'f' in TPT to answer this question.*

- *What did God choose to do in response to human wickedness? Consult verses 3 and 7.*

- *Notice in verse 7 that other creatures besides human beings will bear some of the consequences of divine judgment. From what you have learned so far in Genesis, why do you think animals were included in God's judgment against humanity?*

- *Do you believe that sin always bears consequences beyond the sinner? Why or why not?*

9 SHARE GOD'S HEART

No matter where you live, human beings are not living as they should. Human sin continues. Let's focus on its impact on culture. A culture is "the way of life of a people. It consists of conventional patterns of thought and behavior, including values, beliefs, rules of conduct, political organization, economic activity, and the like, which are passed on from one generation to the next by learning."[69] Reflect on the culture in which you live as you answer the following questions and consider how you can share God's heart with others.

- *What words would you use to describe the moral and spiritual condition of your culture?*

- *What do you think needs to happen in your cultural situation for people to move closer to God rather than farther away?*

- *What role(s) can you play in speaking to your culture's needs and sharing with it the heart of God?*

Divine Salvation and Judgment

In Scripture, salvation and judgment often go hand in hand. For instance, in Exodus, God brings judgment upon Pharaoh and the rest of the Egyptians for enslaving the Hebrews, his chosen people. At the same time, God uses his judgment against Egypt to deliver his people and set them on the way to the promised land (Exodus 3–15). In Genesis, God already passed judgment on Adam and Eve for disobeying him in Eden, but he also preserved their lives and displayed redemption through the shedding of blood and by clothing the human couple with the skins from those slain animals.

When we come to Genesis 6, the human situation seems dire. What God finds could have led to a complete restart in which the total decimation of the human population was warranted. But one man stood out among all the decadence. Through him and his family, God would spare the human race even as he brought judgment on the earth.

Noah, the Man

Book 3 of Genesis (6:9–9:29) focuses on a man named Noah and his family.

- *What characteristics of Noah stood out to God (Genesis 6:9)?*

- *Look through Genesis 5. Who was the only other person named who was close to God? Compare what's said about that person with what's revealed about Noah. What can you conclude from this about how much Noah differed from the rest of the human race?*

- *Genesis 6:8 tells us that, as good as Noah was, it was not his moral character that led God to focus on him. What was it? Consult study note 'h' on this verse in TPT to help inform your answer.*

- *Noah was not a young man. How old was he (5:32)?*

- *Noah was also a family man. Who were his sons (6:10)? Next to each name, write some key information you find in TPT study notes 'a,' 'b,' and 'c' for this verse.*

 EXPERIENCE GOD'S HEART

The biblical description of Noah in comparison to what the rest of humanity was like shows that it is possible to live a life of integrity and obedience to God even in the midst of a corrupt and decadent culture.

- *What do you find is most difficult for you to be or do in the surrounding culture?*

- *How can you overcome the cultural obstacles to growing close to God and following his ways?*

Noah's Mission

Scripture reveals that Yahweh spoke to Noah—the man "who lived close" to him (6:9).

- *First Yahweh told Noah what he was going to do and why (v. 13). Summarize what God said to him.*

- *Next, Yahweh directed Noah to do some construction work (vv. 14–16). What was Noah supposed to build? What were its dimensions? And what other key features did the construction project have?*

 THE EXTRA MILE

Go to the article by Tim Lovett, "Thinking Outside the Box," at https://answersingenesis.org/noahs-ark/thinking-outside-the-box. As you read through it, make notes about Noah's ark that significantly add to your understanding about this ship and its capabilities.

- *Then God told Noah the means he was going to use to bring about his judgment on humankind. What was it, and what was it going to destroy (v. 17)?*

- *Who among humanity would God spare from this coming calamity (v. 18)?*

- *What among the land and sky animals would God also save (vv. 19–20)? And who would be his co-workers in this endeavor?*

- *What provisions did God direct Noah to gather into the ark, and what were they for (v. 21)?*

 # THE EXTRA MILE

Some critics of this historical account claim that the ark would not have been large enough to hold two of every species of animal on earth, pointing out that there are many hundreds of millions of animal species. To this charge, scholars Norman Geisler and Thomas Howe respond:

> First, the modern concept of "species" is not the same as a "kind" in the Bible. There are probably only several hundred different "kinds" of land animals that would have to be taken into the ark. The sea animals stayed in the sea, and many species could have survived in egg form. Second, the ark was not small; it was a huge structure—the size of a modern ocean liner. Furthermore, it had three stories (6:16) which tripled its space to a total of over 1.5 million cubic feet!
> Third, Noah could have taken younger or smaller varieties of some larger animals. Given all of these factors, there was plenty of room for all the animals, food for the trip, and the eight humans aboard.[70]

Even if the biblical "kind" were interpreted as the current scientific meaning of species, Bible scholar Gleason Archer writes that this would not present a problem: "At the present time there are only 290 main species of land animal larger than sheep in size; there are 757 more species ranging in size from sheep to rats, and there are 1,358 smaller than rats. Two of each of these species would fit very comfortably into the cubic capacity of the ark, and leave plenty of room for fodder."[71]

The Answers in Genesis website posts an excellent and more detailed article on this issue. See "How Could All the Animals Fit

on the Ark?," by Michael Belknap and Tim Chaffey, at https://
answersingenesis.org/noahs-ark/how-could-all-animals-fit-ark.

Noah's Response

- *With God's word about judgment and salvation delivered
  to Noah, how did this godly man respond (6:22)?*

- *Was this Noah's typical response to God? To answer, read
  7:5, 8–9, and 16.*

- *Has God ever spoken to you through his Word, a dream,
  a vision, a conversation, or any other means? What did
  he say? Did you obey him? Why or why not?*

Talking It Out

1. Put yourself in Noah's sandals. God comes to you and wants you to prepare for the end of the world as you know it. And his request will commit you to going public in a huge way. Everyone will see what you are building, and they will ask you questions you may find difficult to answer. People may even see you as the crazy religious man or woman who speaks of coming divine judgment while constructing what you claim will be the means of deliverance. What do you imagine your obedience to God would cost you? How might family members, neighbors, religious leaders, the media, and governing officials respond to your claims and activity? How do you think you would handle all the attention and likely derision?

2. Read Hebrews 11, one of the greatest sections in Scripture focused on faith and those who exhibited it so well. Noah is commended here for his faithful obedience to God. Talk about individuals you have heard about or know who have such faith in God. Have any of them become models for you to emulate? What have you learned from them about the life of faith?

3. Noah stood out to Yahweh as godly, marked by integrity, "without fault in his generation," and intimate with him (Genesis 6:9). What do each of these characteristics mean to you? What about them might make an individual stand out in your social circles and culture? Why do you think God prizes these characteristics so highly?

LESSON 10

Judgment through Water, Salvation through Wood

(7:1–9:29)

Noah was around five hundred years of age when God told him about the watery judgment to come (5:32; 6:11–13, 17–18). When the great deluge came, Noah was six hundred years old (7:6). What was he doing for a hundred years? He was faithfully carrying out what God had told him to do: he was building a great ship while upholding his other responsibilities as a family man and engaging with others about his life and work. No doubt he spent a lot of time explaining to others why he was building such a sea-faring vessel (2 Peter 2:5).

In Matthew 24:37–39, Jesus tells us what other people were doing while Noah worked on constructing the ark. They were going about their daily lives "eating, drinking, marrying, and having children. They didn't realize the end was near until Noah entered the ark, and then suddenly, the flood came and took them all away in judgment."

Considering what Jesus said, imagine you were outside of Noah's family just living your life and without any commitment to Yahweh. Down the road a massive construction project was underway—a project unlike anything you had ever seen. Now keep this picture in mind as you answer the following questions.

- *Would the construction work have piqued your curiosity? If so, what would you have done to satisfy your interest?*

- *How do you think you would have responded after learning that the project was an ark designed to survive a worldwide flood? Would you have asked questions to gain more information? Would you have walked away in fear or disbelief? What would you have done?*

- *If you were told that the flood was coming because Yahweh had rendered a verdict on humankind as completely corrupt and unjust and filled with violence, what do you think you would have said or done in response?*

❤ SHARE GOD'S HEART

It's often not easy or comfortable to share God's indictment on humanity. What God told Noah about humanity in his day could easily fit the human race in our time. False religions flourish, hostility toward Christians is escalating, God's moral standards are routinely scorned and dismissed, genocide and slavery are still practiced in different parts of the world, propaganda and lying receive national sanction, and on goes the list of decadence and decay. People don't typically welcome hearing that they are sinful and corrupt, that they are deceived and in need of the truth, and that they are doomed to divine judgment if they fail to repent and put their trust in Jesus Christ. We have good news to share, but many people don't think they need it much less want to hear it.

- *In our day, what are some ways you have shared the good news about Jesus and the salvation he offers?*

- *What responses have you received to what you have shared?*

- *Are you prepared to share the good news knowing that many people will refuse to accept it? Could you endure, as Noah did, knowing what was to come but receiving no favorable responses from those around you except for those of your family?*

When the time was right, God told Noah to take his family and the animals he had collected into the ark.

- *Who was included in Noah's family (Genesis 6:10; 7:7, 13)?*

- *How long were they all in the ark before the floodwaters began (7:7–10)?*

- *How old was Noah at the time (7:11)?*

- *When Noah, his family, and all the animals were safely inside the ark, who closed the ship's door (v. 16; also see TPT study note 'g').*

When the flood began, more than just rain contributed to the waters. "All the fountains of the subterranean deep cracked open and burst up through the ground. Heaven's floodgates were opened, and heavy rains fell on the earth for forty days and forty nights" (vv. 11–12). As Brian Simmons says: "It [was] as though God returned the earth back to the chaos of [Genesis] ch. 1. He once separated the waters and raised up the dry ground; now he was covering the earth again with water and removing the separation that he spoke into existence (see Gen. 1:6–10)."[72] Imagine what it must have been like to have water burst from the ground as it poured down from the sky and to see lakes and rivers break over their banks while sea and ocean water reclaimed beaches and the land that stretched beyond them. The waters that God had once separated, he now allowed to unite in order to bring judgment upon the wickedness of his corrupted image bearers. The massive floodwaters would cleanse a polluted earth.[73]

- *Read Genesis 7:7–8:12. This section of Scripture provides some details about the great flood. Organize these details in a chart, thereby giving you a concise chronology of this incredible event. Suggested headings are provided below. Reproduce, expand, and fill in the chart on separate paper.*

Bible Reference	Event	Date

- *Based on your findings, answer the following questions:*

  For how many days did the rain fall and the waters on and under the earth continue to overcome their boundaries?

  How high did the floodwaters rise?

  How many days did the water cover the earth until it began to recede?

  What was the extent of destruction that the floodwater caused?

  What caused the water to begin to recede?

  Where did the ark come to rest?

  How long did it take for the ground to dry enough so Noah, his family, and the animals could leave the ark?

 EXPERIENCE GOD'S HEART

Read Hebrews 11:7 and what it says about Noah and his faith. Notice how his faithfulness to God saved others, not just himself.

Did you realize that God uses your faith as well to provide for others, not just for you? While he loves you, his reach always extends beyond you. Experience God's heart in your life by cultivating your faith relationship with him, not just for your own sake but for the sake of others he will reach through your faithfulness to him.

- *What are at least one or two steps you can take starting this week to strengthen your faith commitment to God? Put a plan in place to make these steps an habitual part of your walk with him.*

Life Renewed

Worship and Covenant Promise

With God's judgment at an end, Noah and his family could begin life anew.

- *What did Noah do after leaving the ark (8:20)?*

- *How did Yahweh respond to Noah's act of worship (vv. 21–22)?*

God then blessed Noah and his family, and in his blessing, he included some commands for the survivors and all other image bearers to obey.

- *God reiterated what he had first passed along to Adam and Eve (9:1–2; cf. 1:28). What did he say to Noah and his family?*

- *God expanded humanity's food supply. What did it now include that it had not previously (9:3–4; cf. 1:29)?*

- *God also instituted a punishment for human beings to carry out when one of their own was murdered. What was this punishment, and why was it established (9:5–6)?*

- *What was the extent of God's covenant? Did it just include Noah and his family, or did it exceed them (vv. 8–11)?*

- *What was the seal/sign of God's covenant and promise (vv. 12–17)?*

- *Why do you think God continued to repeat his promise that he would never again destroy life on earth through a massive flood?*

Curse and Blessing Going Forward

The remainder of Genesis 9 focuses on Noah and his family while also casting a long view into humanity's future. This section begins by mentioning Noah and his three sons along with one of Noah's grandsons, Canaan, the son of Ham (v. 18). "From these three sons of Noah [Shem, Ham, and Japheth] the entire world was repopulated" (v. 19). In other words, everyone who has been born since is a descendant of one of these three sons. God's command to "reproduce, be fruitful and repopulate the earth" (v. 7) was accomplished through Noah's sons and their descendants.

The biblical account then turns to an event in Noah's life that must have occurred years after he and his family left the ark. For he now had a grandson, and he had learned how to plant a vineyard and make wine from its produce (vv. 20–21). Noah is the first person to develop "viticulture (the science of growing grapes) and viniculture (the science of making wine)." Before this, "the land produces through painful human toil the food for sustenance, but little else. Now he [Noah] subdues the land to produce wine, which uniquely cheers, comforts, and gladdens the heart (Judg. 9:13; Ps. 104:15)."[74]

- *After reaping some of his harvest and producing some wine to enjoy, what happened (Genesis 9:21–23)?*

🎬 THE BACKSTORY

The text says that Ham "gazed on his shamefully exposed father" (Genesis 9:22). The Hebrew word translated "gazed" means "to look at searchingly." Ham didn't just glance at his father's nudity or see him quickly and accidently. Ham stared at him, looking him over. His gaze was voyeuristic. Bruce Waltke points out that

> Voyeurism in general violates another's dignity and robs that one of his or her instinctive desire for privacy and for propriety. It is a form of domination. Ham's, however, is perverse, for his is homosexual voyeurism. Worse yet, he dishonors his father, whom he should have revered in any case (Ex. 21:15–17; Deut. 21:18–21; Mark 7:10), and then increases the dishonor by proclaiming it to others. Ham's brothers thought it sin merely to look at their father's nakedness and took every effort not to do so.[75]

When Noah came out of his stupor and realized what Ham, his youngest son, had done, he cursed Ham's son, Canaan. Now God had already blessed Ham and his brothers just after the flood

(Genesis 9:1). Noah, then, doesn't counter the divine blessing on Ham. Rather, Noah focuses his curse on Ham's son, Canaan. In fact, the curse *and* blessings Noah delivered have the descendants of his three sons in view.

- *What was the curse on Canaan (v.25)? How many times was it pronounced (vv. 26–27)? Why do you think it was repeated after each blessing on Noah's other sons?*

- *In verse 26, the blessing of praise goes to Yahweh, Shem's God, not to Shem, at least not directly. Why do you think this is so? Consider study note 'a' in TPT on this passage.*

- *What blessing does Noah give to Japheth's descendants (v. 27)?*

🏮 THE BACKSTORY

It's important to understand that the curse on Canaan and the blessings on Shem and Japheth are not ethnic as much as they are spiritual. Canaan will become the father of the Canaanites, a people who will possess the promised land and morally and religiously pollute it. Also from Ham and Canaan will come "some of Israel's most bitter enemies: Egypt, Philistia, Assyria, Babylon (see 10:6–13). Behind Noah's prophecy is the concept of corporate solidarity. The ancestors reproduce their own kind…Noah's righteousness is reproduced in Shem and Japheth, his immorality in Ham. The hubris of Ham against his father will be worked out in his descendants, and the modesty of Shem and Japheth in theirs."[76] This doesn't mean that every descendant of Shem and Japheth was modest and moral any more than every descendant of Ham was voyeuristic and immoral. Nevertheless, just as sons and daughters tend to emulate and take on some of the traits of their parents, so would the descendants of Noah's sons. Noah knew what his sons were like, so his prophetic curse and blessings concerned the kind of children he had good reason to believe that his sons would generally produce.

Since Ham and Canaan eventually produced the Canaanites, who did Shem and Japheth produce? Israel came from Shem, as did the Messiah (Luke 3:36). In his blessing on Shem, Noah identified his son by his relationship with God, using the covenant name Yahweh (Genesis 9:26). "This is the first indication that God elects the line of Shem to rule the earth (Gen. 1:26–28) and crush the Serpent (Gen. 3:15; 4:26). Sovereign grace always opens a blessed future, as when God chooses as Shem's successors, Abraham, not Nahor; Isaac, not Ishmael; Jacob, not Esau; Judah, not Joseph."[77]

From Japheth eventually come the Greeks and Romans.

Since the death and resurrection of Jesus Christ (a Shemite), all who are in him by faith "share in the blessing of Shem" and, spiritually speaking, "make their homes among the tents of Shem" (9:27). Moreover, even ethnicity has been overcome for those who are in Christ. "Today his church includes the Ethiopian eunuch

(Ham), Peter and Paul (Shem), and Cornelius (Japheth). God is no respecter of a person's ethnic origin but of his or her spiritual condition. In God's household, none is unclean (Acts 10), and in Christ there is neither Jew nor Greek, for all are Abraham's [spiritual] seed (Gal. 3:26–29)."[78]

Finally, when in history did Canaan's descendants become subservient to the descendants of Shem and Japheth? Bible scholar Allen Ross explains:

> The enslavement of Canaanites is seen in many situations in the history of the Old Testament...The Canaanites were defeated and enslaved by eastern kings [Gen. 14]. Another example was the Gibeonites who later under Joshua became wood choppers and water carriers for Israel's tabernacle (Josh. 9:27). If the subjugation of Canaan to Japheth's line is to be carried to the extreme...then it would go no further than the Battle of Carthage (146 b.c.) where the Phoenicians (who were Canaanites) were finally defeated...
>
> ...The Canaanites would have to be dispossessed from their place by Israel under Joshua in order for blessing to come on Shem [Gen. 9:26] and for the Japhethites to dwell in the tents of Shem. This meant that the Japhethites would live with the Shemites on friendly terms, not that the Japhethites would dispossess the Shemites. So verses 24–29 actually set the foundation for Israel's foreign policy in the [promised] land (Deut. 20:16–18).[79]

Genesis 9 closes with the end of Noah's very long life.

- *Read Genesis 9:28–29. How long did Noah live after the flood? What was the entire length of his life?*

- *Noah suffered the same fate as all of his ancestors except for one. Who was the lone exception (5:24)?*

From Noah to Jesus and Beyond

The New Testament looks back on Noah as an exemplar of faith and righteousness (Hebrews 11:7; 2 Peter 2:5). And Jesus compared his second coming to life just before the flood. Just as the flood took people by surprise and doomed them all but a few, so Jesus' coming will be unexpected by the many, and salvation from judgment will come to only those who have already put their faith in him (Matthew 24:36–51; Luke 17:26–36).

The great flood event in Genesis is a story of

catastrophic destruction that proves God's
hatred of sin, a picture of the wrath of God
that will be finally revealed at the last day
on all who ignore his demands and go

their own way. But it also offers comfort: God will continue to uphold the present natural order "as long as the earth exists," despite man's incorrigible perverseness of heart. More than that, it gives assurance to the righteous, those who walk with God and keep his commandments, that in the last great day, or in the natural disasters that presage it, they too will be preserved unto eternal life.[80]

Talking It Out

1. The great flood that inundated the earth is an early reminder in Scripture that God, while patient, will not endure human wickedness forever. One day he will bring it to an end, even to an ultimate close as the book of Revelation makes crystal clear. In the meantime, is God involved in the world by curbing and judging sin? If so, how? Provide a few examples within the pages of Scripture and outside of it that reveal God's ongoing judgment on human corruption.

2. The flood account also shows that God saves. He spared Noah and his family and various kinds of animals through a devastating judgment. And then he promised that he would never again judge the world in that way. What do these sides

of the story tell you about the value Yahweh places on his creation, especially on his image bearers? Does he think they are simply garbage, throwaways that mean nothing, that have lost any significance they once had? What do you think? And how does your answer relate to how God regards you?

3. God established the rainbow as the sign of his pledge to never again destroy life on earth through massive floodwaters. What are some other promises God has made that also came with a sign of his pledge? As just one example, compare John 16:7–15 with Acts 2. What was the sign that Jesus had kept his promise? Can you think of other cases? Has God done this for you?

4. Noah's obedience to Yahweh is repeated and emphasized in Genesis 6–9. His obedience is contrasted with the disobedience of almost everyone else on earth. What was Noah's reward for his faithfulness to God? What did the unfaithful receive for their disobedience? Which group do you want to follow and emulate? What are some ways you can do that?

LESSON 11

New Families and Dispersed Nations

(10:1–32)

The story of the great, worldwide flood ends with Noah, his three sons, their wives, and at least one adult grandchild. They are doing their part to subdue the earth and populate it perhaps somewhere near where the ark came to rest. Genesis 10 starts Book 4 (10:1–11:9) and tells us about some of the many descendants of Noah's sons, including where they traveled and settled. Chapter 11 reveals why these descendants did not stay together, why they scattered so far geographically from one another. As we'll see, chapter 10 shows that these families continued to reproduce and fill the earth as God had commanded them to. Chapter 11, however, makes it clear that their great dispersion did not occur out of obedience to Yahweh. Just as divine judgment followed Adam and Eve's disobedience, Cain's murder of Abel, demonically influenced marriages, and humanity's many other perversions and corruptions, so God would bring judgment upon the descendants of Noah for their out-of-control hubris.

The floodwaters had not changed the basic condition of humankind—a condition that had changed for the worse since the original couple's sin in Eden. But God still had a redemptive plan in place, and he would carry it out despite humanity's ongoing attempts to move beyond their image bearing status and become gods themselves.

The Table of Nations

Genesis 10 is often referred to as the table of nations. It "represents the nations as of one blood, multiplying under God's blessing as distinct tribes and nations."[81] We are all children of Adam and Noah. Adam and Eve began populating the earth after their exile from Eden, and Noah and his sons, along with their wives, began repopulating earth after the flood. We have one origin. We share the same blood. We are of one race—the human race. As the great theologian Augustine said in the early fifth century, "From one man, whom God created as the first, the whole human race descended, according to the faith of Holy Scripture."[82]

As we'll see, "the table [of nations] is not concerned with a simple list of the sons of the ancestors [that is, Noah's sons]; rather, it is concerned with tracing 'what became of' these sons... The passage is focusing on the great development and movement of families that were of interest to Israel."[83]

The Table's Structure

Genesis 10 orders the specifics about individuals, families, tribes, cities, and nations using a clear and well-organized structure. It uses this structure to trace "tribal relationships back to ancestral connections in the remote past, from whom the nations of the earth developed."[84] Through this, the writer shows the common origin of the world's post-flood families and nations and connects them to the three sons God had blessed.

First, the table's structure begins with a heading (v. 1) and closes with a summary statement about dispersion (v. 32).

- *The heading (v. 1) is the toledot statement that starts this section of Genesis. What does it tell you about what's to come in the passages that follow?*

- *Verse 32 provides the wrap-up of the table of nations. What does it say about the content that preceded it?*

Following the table's heading, three sections occur, each with the same basic structure, and each laying out details about Noah's sons' descendants. You'll find the first of these sections laid out and filled out below. Following it, see if you can fill in the missing information under Ham and Shem.

1. Japheth

Heading: "The sons of Japheth..." (v. 2).

Expansion: "The sons of Gomer..." (v. 3).

"The sons of Javan..." (v. 4).

Dispersion: "All of Japheth's descendants lived in their respective tribes and regions, each group speaking its own language. From there, the people spread to distant shores and faraway lands" (v. 5).

2. Ham

Heading:

Expansion:

Dispersion:

3. Shem

Heading:

Expansion:

Dispersion:

Look at the dispersion statements again. The key elements of them for Ham and Shem are the same but Japheth's is different:

Japheth: tribes, regions, language, people (nations)

Ham: families, lands, languages, nations

Shem: families, lands, languages, nations

There's one more thing to mention about structure in Genesis 10: it has numerical symmetry and significance.

How many sons of Japheth are listed (v. 2)?

What is the total number of sons for two of Japheth's, Gomer and Javan (vv. 3–4)?

Count up the number of Ham's descendants (vv. 6–8, 13–18). How many are listed?

Do the same with Shem's descendants (vv. 21–30). How many did you find?

If you add Ham's and Shem's descendants together, what is the total?

Bible scholar Allen Ross comments on these numbers:

> Of the sons of Japheth, who number seven, two are selected for further listing. From those two sons come seven grandsons, completing a selective list of fourteen names under Japheth. With Ham's thirty descendants and Shem's twenty-six, the grand total is seventy. [Hebrew scholar] Cassuto believes that this total is an attempt to show that the placing of the nations around Israel (which is not listed) is by divine providence. He suggests that the seventy nations correspond to the number of the families of Israel, for God arranged their boundaries according to the number of the Israelites (Deut. 32:8).[85]

These structural characteristics of the table of nations show how tightly woven this section of Scripture is and why it matters.

Seventy nations are dispersed, all of which come out of Noah's family—the ones God saved from global catastrophe and divine judgment. Before the Hebrews go into the promised land under Joshua, they are a collection of seventy large families, all of whom are the fruit of God's liberation work for his people from Egyptian slavery (Exodus 13:2, 14–15; Deuteronomy 32:8). He will bless them in new land and through them bring blessing to the other nations, which includes the knowledge and fear of the true God (Genesis 12:1–3; 17:6–8; Joshua 4:23–24). Jumping to the New Testament, Jesus appoints seventy of his followers to "go ahead of him into every town he was about to visit" because, as he told them, "The harvest is huge [and] there are not enough harvesters to bring it in" (Luke 10:1–2). Jesus has no desire for just a select few to know the truth and find life. He strives to expand the gospel message as far as he can.

In other words, from creation to Jesus, God's love has always reached from his people to the nations. He is sovereign over all, and he has judgment over all, but he also has an eternal desire to bless them. He saves so the saved can turn around and reach out to others. We, his people, are blessed to be a blessing to others (1 Timothy 2:1–8).

♥ SHARE GOD'S HEART

- *Everyone is from a nation. What nation do you now live in? Have you always lived there? How about other family members? Do you know from where they came? If so, name the nation(s).*

- *No matter the country you are from, God loves you and wants to bless you. Take some time to thank him for his devotion to you.*

- *Since you are blessed to bless others, who can you bless in your family, your neighborhood, your workplace, your church, or somewhere else in your nation? Ask God to help you come up with a way to love, encourage, inspire, comfort, or in other ways bless that person within the next week or two.*

· *Finally, go before God again and ask him to guide you in how you can bless a nation other than your own. You can focus on an individual or family there, a church or parachurch organization, a missionary, or a specific charity. The opportunities are numerous and varied. You can bless through prayer, financial gifts, food or clothing contributions, correspondence, or by offering your knowledge or skills. Partner with God. Let him show you how you can share his heart with others.*

The Table's Specifics

The structure of Genesis 10 organizes the names of individuals, tribes, and places, all of which came from the three sons of Noah. To us it may seem odd that phrases such as "sons of" and "fathers of" could introduce families, tribes, cities, and nations, not just individuals. But in the ancient world, "terms of family relationships [were often used] to denote political and civic relationships: a father was a more powerful nation, a son was a dependent tribe, brothers were allies, and daughters were suburbs."[86] Family relationship terms could also be used to designate the founder or important ancestor of, say, a tribe, city, or nation. When in the United States we refer to George Washington as the father of the nation, we are using the word "father" in the same way Moses sometimes did.

So Moses traces significant groups and places to their ancestral beginnings in Shem, Ham, and Japheth. His list does not claim to be exhaustive, listing every people group and nation in the post-flood world. But it does name "the major peoples known to Israel and their relationship to each other and to Israel."[87] Remember, Genesis is the first book of the Torah—ultimately designed as one of the five most important divinely revealed books for the establishment and direction of the nation God would father as his own. Genesis 10, then, focuses on the nations that would be most important to the Hebrews as they prepared to conquer the land that God had set aside for them.

Individuals

In Genesis 10, the named individuals are Noah, Shem, Ham, Japheth, Canaan, Ashkenaz, Riphath, Cush, Nimrod, Sabteca, Eber, Elam, Arphaxad, Lud, Aram, Uz, Hul, Gether, Mash, Peleg, Joktan, Almodad, Jerah, Hadoram, Abimael, and Ophir.

- *Select one or more of these individuals and conduct some research on them. TPT's study notes are a good place to start. You can also consult a Bible dictionary or Bible encyclopedia, a commentary on Genesis, or an online resource such as biblegateway.com or biblehub. com. Along with the many things you may discover about the individual you choose, see if you can answer the following questions:*

    Did this individual walk with God?

    What do we know about this person's character and lifestyle?

Where did this person live?

What was the fruit (good or bad) of this person's life?

 EXPERIENCE GOD'S HEART

God cares about families and their individual members. How much do you know about your family members, including relatives such as aunts and uncles and cousins? Part of loving others is taking time to get to know them. Start with those closest to you. Select a family member about whom you know little or would like to know more. Ask him or her questions about their life history, life-changing experiences, and views about God, Jesus, and anyone or anything else that comes to mind. Don't make this an "interview," rather follow the conversation wherever it goes. Your goal is to learn so you can love this person better. Also pray for this family member, asking God how you can show his love to this person.

Tribes/Nations

There are a number of plural nouns in the list that indicate tribes or nations, not individuals. Names with gentilic endings (—ites) depict tribes as well, along with the names of cities and territories in which they lived or founded. These names include Cyprus, Rhodes, Egypt, Madai, Javan, Tiras, Ethiopia, Ludites, Anamites,

Lehabites, Naphtuhites, Pathrusites, Casluhites, Caphtorites, Philistines, Hittites, Canaanites, Jebusites, Amorites, Girgashites, Hivites, Arkites, Sinites, Arvadites, Zemarites, Hamathites, Shelah, and Sheleph.

- *Choose one or more of these tribal groups and see what you can find out about them. Begin with TPT's study notes and then branch out to another Bible resource, such as a Bible dictionary or encyclopedia, a commentary, or an online resource such as biblegateway.com or biblehub.com. Take notes on what you find. Also see if you can answer any of the following questions:*

  Where was the tribe/nation located?

  What was the tribe's/nation's reputation? Were they honored, feared, or easily controlled?

  What happened to them? Did they die out, become a great nation or people, or contribute anything of lasting value to humanity?

Places

The table also cites many geographical locations, among which are Mesha, Sephar, Tubal, Togarmah, Seba, Sabtah, Dedan, Gomer, Magog, Assyria (which also became the name of a feared nation), Mesheck, Tarshish, Elishah, Havilah, Shinar, Sheba, Hazarmaveth, Diklah, Obal, Havilah, and Jobab. Along with these are the names of known cities: Babel, Erech, Akkad, Calneh, Sidon, Raamah, Ninevah, Rehoboth-Ir, Calah, Resen, and Uzal. In Genesis 10:19, Moses also provides the boundaries of the territory in which Canaan's descendants settled. The boundaries were the cities Sidon, Gerar, Gaza, Sodom, Gomorrah, Admah, Zeboiim, and Lasha. God will later designate this land for his chosen people, the Hebrews, who will descend from the seed of Abraham.

- *Choose at least one of these geographical sites to learn more about. Research others if you have the time and interest. Start with TPT's study notes and then consult another Bible resource, some of which we've already mentioned. As you take notes on your chosen place, try to answer as many of the following questions as you can:*

Where was your chosen place found in the ancient world?

How far was this place situated to what would later become Israel? Also, was it east, west, south, or north of the territory Israel eventually occupied?

Is the place mentioned elsewhere in Scripture? If so, where and what is said about it?

The Dispersion of Nations Overall

Although we don't have enough information to locate every name mentioned in the table of nations, Bible scholars have enough writings and artifacts from history to know with varying degrees of certainty where the descendants of Ham, Shem, and Japheth settled and grew in the ancient world. For the most part, Japheth's descendants dispersed to Syria, Assyria, Asia Minor, the land around and between the Black Sea and Caspian Sea, the Greek islands in the Mediterranean Sea, and Europe, all the way west to Spain; Ham's progenies largely settled in Arabia, modern-day Iraq, Assyria, Crete, Canaan, and northern and eastern Africa, including Egypt and Ethiopia; and Shem's descendants settled parts of Assyria, Babylonia, and southern Arabia.

Key Individuals

Along with Shem, Ham, and Japheth, the table of nations mentions three other individuals who deserve special attention: Nimrod, Eber, and Peleg.

Nimrod

Nimrod gets five verses (vv. 8–12). They speak to his deeds and reputation.

- *Nimrod was part of whose genealogy—Shem's, Ham's, or Japheth's?*

- *Nimrod's reputation comes through descriptions about him (vv. 8–9). What are these descriptions, and did Yahweh agree with them?*

- *Now check out TPT study note 'm' for verse 9. What information does this give that you would add to your previous answer?*

- *To gain even more insight into Nimrod and his influence as a kingdom builder, conduct some research on Babel (v. 10) and Nineveh (v. 11). Go to one or more of the kinds of Bible resources we have already mentioned. Also consult the TPT study notes on these sites. What did you learn about these places? What were their reputations? In what ways do they reflect their founder, Nimrod?*

Eber

- *From whom did Eber ultimately descend—Shem, Ham, or Japheth (v. 21)?*

- *Which people group ultimately came from Eber (v. 21)?*

 WORD WEALTH

The Hebrew word *eber* is the root of the word *Hebrew*. Or, another way of looking at this, *Hebrew* is the gentilic form of the word *eber*. Genesis 10:21 introduces the great ancestor of the Hebrew people, Eber, and identifies him as coming from Shem's line.[88] The path of the chosen seed predicted in Genesis 3:15 continued to narrow.

Moreover, as Waltke explains:

> This genealogy accents Eber by mentioning him out of order..., by repeating his name as son of Shelah and as father of Peleg and Joktan, and by mentioning at the outset that Shem is the father of all his sons. The narrator does this because Eber is the last ancestor in the in-depth lineage from Shem to Abraham before the division between his sons into the nonelect through Joktan and the elect through Peleg.[89]

Peleg

- *In which of Noah's sons' lines is Peleg (10:25)?*

- *What does Peleg's name mean? To answer this, see verse 25 and TPT study note 't.'*

WORD WEALTH

Genesis 10 reveals from whom and to where the earth's peoples dispersed after the flood. Genesis 11 reveals why this dispersion occurred. Chapter 10 hints at the "why" that chapter 11 presents when it refers to the languages of the dispersed peoples (10:5, 20, 31). Chapter 11 explains why the different human languages came about.

Another hint is provided by the meaning of Peleg. *Peleg* comes from the Hebrew root word that means "to divide." "Like many biblical names, this is prophetic in that it foreshadows the great events that would take place in Peleg's lifetime."[90] Among these great events would be the division of human language and the dispersion of human families and tribes over the earth. Another great event would be "the separation of the elect line of Shem from the nonelect line."[91]

According to Allen Ross, since the division of language happened in Peleg's lifetime, "the [Tower of] Babel event occurred five generations after the Flood."[92]

Talking It Out

1. People often talk about human diversity and the need for equality and unity, but they rarely define these ideas, and all the talk usually ends up fostering division and confusion more than anything else. Consider the teaching of Genesis 1 about all human beings as image bearers, sharing the same human nature, and then add to that this book's teaching on human origins—that all of us are descendants of Adam and Eve (Genesis 4–5) and Noah and his sons (Genesis 10). What are the implications of these truths when applied to the current talk on humanity and our relationships with one another?

2. The Creator is not just the God of Israel or the church but the God over all peoples and nations, whether or not they acknowledge him or commit their lives to him. This has been the case since the beginning of human history. While God has given them great freedom, he also holds them responsible for the use of their freedom. He also intercedes in ways and times of his choice, thereby exercising his freedom and authority over his creation. How should these truths direct the way we should view and relate to others, both those within our people group and nation and those without, including those who reject these truths?

3. The Table of Nations lists places, not just people. Throughout Genesis and the rest of Scripture, a number of places take on incredible importance. List some of the places you recall from your study of the Bible and then go online or to a printed Bible resource to learn more about one or two of them. Tell someone else about what you discovered, including what made that place significant in biblical history.

4. Since biblical times, the gospel of Christ has gone out into all the world, reaching peoples and nations unknown to the Hebrew prophets and Jesus' apostles. Select a people group or nation and learn more about when and how they first heard the gospel, how they have received it, and how they acted upon it. Commit to joining with at least one other believer to pray for these people. One day, your prayers will bear the fruit of seeing individuals from among them joining with people from other tribes, languages, people groups, and nations singing praises to the Lamb of God around his throne (Revelation 5:9–10).

LESSON 12

The Tower of Babel

(11:1–9)

Have you ever wondered why there are so many different languages throughout the world? According to Genesis, human life did not begin this way. The one human race spoke one shared language, though we don't know what it was. The great flood of judgment did not alter this fact, but another judgment did.

The Post-Flood Situation

At the end of Genesis 10, we're told, "After the flood, Noah's descendants formed nations as the people spread throughout the earth" (10:32). And these dispersed people already spoke different languages. How did this situation arise? Genesis 11, the story of the Tower of Babel, offers the explanation.

- *Genesis 11:1 gives us a key piece of information about human language at this time. What is that fact?*

- *Before the dispersion of people groups detailed in Genesis 10, chapter 11 says that people were migrating in what direction (11:2)? In what land did they settle?*

THE BACKSTORY

The plain of Shinar (v. 2) was in southern Mesopotamia. At this time in history and even many centuries later, this area was celebrated by the Babylonians, Greeks, and Romans "as a region of prodigious fertility." Furthermore:

> Before the fourth millennium b.c., a non-Semitic people known as the Sumerians entered this fertile region and developed a high degree of civilization and a pictograph cuneiform writing that was the precursor of Semitic cuneiform. Isaiah named Shinar as one of the places from which the Jews would be regathered at the end time (Isa. 11:11). Zechariah 5:11 mentions Shinar in connection with the woman and the ephah, symbolizing the spirit of godless commercialism as originating in Babylon. Nebuchadnezzar carried away Temple treasures taken from Jerusalem to the Shinar area (Dan. 1:2).[93]

Shinar was a great choice for people to settle. But at the time of history that Genesis 11 records, it also turned out to be a place of tremendous upheaval.

- *Once the people were in Shinar, what did they decide to do (Genesis 11:3–4)?*

- *Given what the text records, did the people engage in this great construction project to glorify God or themselves? Explain.*

- *Was their plan to build a settlement in Shinar and then branch out from there? Or did they plan to stay in Shinar and flourish there? Did their choice show obedience to God's directives to their ancestors, or did it show disobedience (see 9:1, 7)?*

- *Although the people wanted to build a tower that would rise "into the heavens" (11:4), what did Yahweh do in order to even see their tower (v. 5)?*

⚡ DIGGING DEEPER

The words "Yahweh came down to see" (v. 5) raise an issue about talk of God that occurs quite often in Scripture. When speaking about God, the biblical writers frequently use different types of analogical language in order to communicate truths about who God is, what he is like, and how he works. Analogy expresses a similarity between things while at least implicitly acknowledging important differences between them. The writers use analogy because we cannot grasp God any other way. Since God is unlimited (infinite) in all he is, we who are limited (finite) cannot comprehend him in his fullness (1 Kings 8:27; Job 11:7–11). For instance, we understand what it means to know something, so we can have a basic idea what it means for God to know something. But that God knows something inside and out, that nothing is hidden from him or unknown to him, that he knows everything in an absolutely unlimited way—well, that depth and breadth of knowledge is too much for us to comprehend (Romans 11:33–36). This is where analogical language comes in. As God's image bearers, we know we are like God. So we, for example, know things, will things, and feel things, and God does too. But he does all of these things infinitely and perfectly and sinlessly, while we do not. We, then, are like God in some ways, but he is not like us. Everything we are, we are finitely, while everything God is, he is infinitely.

We can compare ourselves to him in some ways, but he is so far beyond us in what he is that the comparison breaks down. Finite language cannot fully express infinite truths any more than finite creatures can fully resemble the infinite Creator.[94]

Now let's go back to the imagery of God descending so he could see the construction work going on in the land of Shinar. Since God knows absolutely everything, he doesn't learn anything. He didn't have to come down from anywhere to know what was happening in Shinar. Moses uses this imagery, not to communicate to us that God needed to see for himself what he already knew, but to make the point that the design to build the tower so it reached into the heavens was such a puny and futile endeavor that God had to "descend" in order to even see it. Moses uses figurative (that is, anthropomorphic language, which is a type of analogy) to reveal God's assessment of the builders' ridiculous efforts.[95]

- *What is Yahweh's response to the builders' efforts, and why does he make it (Genesis 11:6)?*

- *Did you notice the use of "us" in God's response? Compare it to a couple of other uses of such plural language in Genesis (1:26; 3:22). Who do you think constitutes "us" in 11:7?*

- *Was Yahweh's response to the building project effective (11:8–9)? Explain your answer.*

- *Why do you think God's counteraction worked?*

 DIGGING DEEPER

When God confused human language and that led to people scattering "over the face of the earth" (v. 9), it likely didn't mean that each person spoke a different language than each other person. Rather, it's more likely that God allowed each group—such as a family and tribe—to speak the same language while changing up the languages of other groups. The statements in Genesis 10 about "each group speaking its own language" (v. 5; cf. vv. 20, 31) would support this interpretation. So the members of each group still understood each other, which is why they stayed together, moved together, and flourished together.

Moreover, God bringing an end to all human beings speaking the same language was not a consequence of him somehow fearing them, as if anything his creatures do could threaten the all-powerful, sovereign Creator. Instead, God acted to restrain human sin while judging it. The people thought they could force their way into the heavens, make themselves gods. Collectively, they believed they could take dominion of earth *and* heaven on their own, bring all of reality under their own power and authority. Not content with delegated sovereignty as granted by God, they wanted total sovereignty. But as Henri Blocher comments, the Babel approach at any time of history is wrong and a dead end:

> The pride of Babel is doomed to *failure*. The judgment that strikes the imperial, totalitarian enterprise is the outcome that runs totally counter to the aims it had set itself. The tower remains unfinished, the target of the jibes of all who pass by it; these are the men who began to build and who were unable to finish (*cf.* Lk. 14:29f.). The union attempted by force brings about division and dispersion. The claim to reach up to heaven sinks in confusion. The derision of the Lord, who laughs at presumptuous conspirators (Ps. 2:4), emerges in the word-play on the name Babel. Whilst the Babylonians gave it the meaning "Gate of God' (*Bab-ili*), Genesis links it with *balal*, the root of the word for 'confusion', like our 'blah-blah-blah'.
>
> The ridiculous failure of Babel signifies the failure of all totalitarian attempts. No human system manages to encompass everything; there always persists the irreducible element which sows the seed of rebellion and condemns the tyranny of the masters and of the thought controllers. Even the most complete of these systems, the totalitarianism of the final Babylon, the antichrist, will not be able to realize its mad imperialist design; only its sins will be 'heaped *high as heaven*' (Rev. 18:5). If

it seems to succeed at first, the System is
able, in proportion to its success, merely
to create confusion. Only the supremacy of
the God of heaven permits unity and order.[96]

By his gracious judgment on Babel, Yahweh gets in the definitive word on human pride. No matter what we do to try to circum-
vent God, resist him, defy him, or even assault him, he will have
the last word, not us. And our feeble attempts against him will end
in confusion and defeat.

Fortunately, Babel is not the last word on human history. God
will keep working out his plan to bless humanity and not leave
them mired in their own sin and corruption.

◆ EXPERIENCE GOD'S HEART

- *Divine judgment (which includes God's correction,
  discipline, and rebuke) always comes with a benefit for
  those who have eyes to discern it and the humility to
  receive it and act on it. Describe a time in your life when
  this happened to you and what you learned from it.*

- *Have you shared this story with another person? If so,
  why, and what was the outcome?*

- *Turn your heart heavenward and offer your gratitude to your divine Lover, thanking him for restraining and correcting you when needed and not abandoning you to the sin that so easily corrupts and diminishes your life.*

❤ SHARE GOD'S HEART

Since the confusion of human language at the Tower of Babel, even more languages have developed. In fact, there are so many of them that no one person can learn them all. Even learning to read, speak, and understand our own language well is difficult, and then using it to clearly communicate our thoughts, experiences, dreams, desires, and actions to others offers its own challenges. It's much easier to be misunderstood than it is for someone to accurately grasp what we are saying. Sometimes we struggle even to find the words to express what we wish to say.

God, however, is the author of language. The Son of God is even described as "the Living Expression" (John 1:1), which goes beyond mere linguistics but also includes it. As Brian Simmons says, "Jesus Christ is the eternal Message, the creative Word, and the Living Expression of God made visible. He is the divine self-expression of all that God is, contains, and reveals in incarnated flesh. Just as we express ourselves in words, God has perfectly expressed himself in Christ."[97]

- *Consider how you can use your words to tell others about the living, creative Word of God. And remember, just as the Living Expression of God is more than words, so should your life express him in more than words. The content and tone of our speech should represent, resemble, and reveal the One we talk about, which requires that our character image him. Look up the following passages and write down what you learn there.*

Ephesians 4:29–31

Colossians 4:5–6

- *Now go to the Living Expression, Jesus Christ, and ask him to work within you to help you make the counsel in these texts an habitual part of your life, knowing that this will not only enlarge and enrich your life as an image bearer but will also make your relationships with others more Christlike too.*

A Look Back and Ahead

In eleven chapters, Genesis has taken us from the origin of the universe to the earth's cleansing with water, from the creation of image bearers to their exile from Paradise and their proliferation far beyond those borders, from the first murder to demonically influenced marriages, from the promise of a Conqueror to the separating of the chosen seed from the unchosen seed. Human life has blossomed, and human sin has become more corruptive. Through all of this, God has blessed and saved even as he has judged.

In the second part of the study guide that covers the rest of Genesis, human history continues to unfold, with God narrowing the chosen line to one man, Abraham, in order to bring blessing to the entire human race. It's here that we will learn about the fathers of the nation that came to be known as Israel. It's also in this section of Genesis that God's caring, gracious, and just providence over the nations of the earth becomes ever more clear. The Creator has not left his creation to struggle on its own. He has a plan for it, and human sin will not thwart it!

Talking It Out

1. The confusion of human languages is divinely reversed and answered in Acts 2. Read Acts 1–2 and compare them to Genesis 10 and 11. Unlike the post-flood peoples who attempted to rival God, what were the first followers of Jesus doing? Were they obeying their Master? And when the Spirit came upon them in Acts 2, what effect did he have on them and on those who heard them? Especially focus on the Spirit's influence on human language. What does all of this tell you about God's sovereignty over human affairs? What does it reveal about the consequences of human obedience and disobedience?

2. Various groups throughout history have tried to create their own empires and all have eventually failed. Among these are the Aztecs, the Persians, the Assyrians, the Romans, the Mongolians, the British, the French, the Spanish, the Germans, the Japanese, the Russians, and the Chinese. Some of these empires completely collapsed, while others were pushed back or dwindled into much smaller national borders. What do these attempts reveal about the divine limits set on human pride and ambition?

3. The Tower of Babel story introduces a city in human history that the Bible routinely views as "the embodiment of human pride and godlessness that must attract the judgment of almighty God" (see also Isaiah 13–14).[98] In contrast is the city of Jerusalem, which one day God will establish as the eternal city, triumphing over the wickedness of Babylon and all it symbolizes (Revelation 18; 21). Regardless of how much evil seems to prevail and succeed, we can be confident that the God of the universe will bring it to an end and fully unite his people and set them in a world free of sin, death, and the devil. Imagine what such a world will be like, and then offer your praise to Yahweh for faithfully and sovereignly continuing to execute his plan of salvation and judgment.

APPENDIX 1

The Big Bang and Creation

Christians accept biblical teaching because it comes from God, the One who is truth, the One who cannot lie (Isaiah 65:16; Psalm 119:160; 1 Samuel 15:29; Titus 1:1–2; Hebrews 6:18). Among the teachings of Scripture is creation *ex nihilo*. God created the entire universe "from nothing." No pre-existent stuff was there. Eternally, God was and is and always will be. Then something came to be that was not God, and he caused it to be. This new thing was the universe itself. Also, Genesis revealed this picture of God speaking and then what he declared coming to be—creation *ex nihilo*. Christians have accepted this teaching and taught it throughout church history.

For a long time, however, apart from a handful of philosophical arguments against the notion of an eternal universe,[99] the discipline of science could not confirm or deny this biblical teaching about the beginning of the universe. In fact, some scientists argued that the universe had always existed virtually unchanged. Apart from biological evolution and the emergence of life, the universe as a whole remained in a steady state of existence.

Scientific findings in the twentieth century radically changed this view of the universe. Astronomer Robert Jastrow in his book *God and Astronomers* prefaced his discussion of these findings with a bold claim:

> Now we see how the astronomical
> evidence leads to a biblical view of the
> origin of the world. The details differ, but
> the essential elements in the astronomical
> and biblical accounts of Genesis are the

same: the chain of events leading to man commenced suddenly and sharply at a definite moment in time, in a flash of light and energy.[100]

Jastrow's book surveys the discoveries that led to what's called the Big Bang theory of the origin of the universe. This is how some scientists described this theory in the journal *Scientific American*:

> The universe began from a state of infinite density. Space and time were created in that event and so was all the matter in the universe. It is not meaningful to ask what happened before the big bang; it is somewhat like asking what is north of the north pole. Similarly, it is not sensible to ask where the big bang took place. The point-universe was not an object isolated in space; it was the entire universe, and so the only answer can be that the big bang happened everywhere.[101]

In other words, at some point in the remote past, there was absolutely nothing. Then, in a flash of light and energy, the universe exploded into existence. At that incredible moment, time, space, and matter came into being—all at once!

What's the evidence for this amazing event? Jastrow explains the most significant scientific discoveries in *God and the Astronomers*. When he wrote his book, he was a professed "agnostic in religious matters," [102] and he found the evidence for the Big Bang compelling. Here's a summary of some of the evidence he presents.

First, in 1913, scientist Vesto Slipher "discovered that about a dozen galaxies in our vicinity were moving away from the earth at very high speeds, ranging up to two million miles per hour."[103] This suggested that the universe was expanding. Other scientists confirmed Slipher's discovery. In the meantime, Slipher kept working, and by 1925 "he had clocked the velocities of 42 galaxies. Nearly all were retreating from the earth at high speeds."[104] What did this suggest? What was making every galaxy move away from every other galaxy? Could it have been the result of a cosmic explosion?

Second, in 1915, physicist Albert Einstein presented his theory of general relativity. One of its surprising implications, an implication Einstein didn't himself realize, is that it

> led to the surprising result that everything in the universe is simultaneously expanding and decelerating. The only physical phenomenon in which expansion and deceleration occur at the same time is an explosion. But if the universe is the aftermath of an explosion, then sometime in the past it must have had a beginning. There must have been a moment at which the explosion began. If it had a beginning, then through the principle of cause and effect this beginning implies the existence of a Beginner.[105]

Third, beginning around 1928, after Slipher moved on to other work, astronomers Edwin Hubble and later Milton Humason began investigating what Slipher had discovered, but this time using bigger and more sophisticated instruments. Humason clocked the speeds of many galaxies that Slipher had been unable to detect. Humason "probed the depths of space out to a distance of more than 100 million light years." He found that every galaxy was "moving away from the earth at a high speed. Some were retreating at the extraordinary speed of 100 million miles an hour."[106] Hubble then came up with a way to measure the distances of the various galaxies. His calculations of about a dozen nearby galaxies determined that the "majority were more than a million light years away, and the distance to the farthest one was seven million light years." That's a staggering distance when you realize that a single light year is six trillion miles. Hubble then "plotted speed against distance on a sheet of graph paper, and arrived at the amazing relationship known as Hubble's law: *the farther away a galaxy is, the faster it moves.* This is the law of the expanding Universe...Now both theory and observation pointed to an expanding Universe and a beginning in time."[107]

Fourth, scientists began discussing how the second law of thermodynamics might apply to the universe. In the mid-1850s, a German mathematical physicist named Rudolf Clausius formulated this law. When applied to the universe, the law can be stated this way: "In a closed, isolated system, the amount of usable energy in the universe is decreasing."[108] Consider a bathtub. If you fill it with hot water, the water will gradually cool. The energy that made it hot at first decreases until the water reaches a state of equilibrium. Unless more energy is injected into the water, its temperature will remain unchanged. Or think about a watch that you have to wind up. It will run fine for a while, but eventually it will run down until it stops. It has run out of usable energy. Well, this second law of thermodynamics also applies to the largest system with mass and energy that we know about—the universe. If all of the galaxies in the universe are expanding away from each other, the energy that generated that expansion won't last forever. It will gradually wind down until the universe reaches a state of equilibrium. So the question scientists began to pose was this: If the universe is winding down, when was it wound up, and who or what wound it up?

Fifth, scientists discovered that the universe is bathed in a glow of radiation. Jastrow explains:

> In 1965 Arno Penzias and Robert Wilson
> of Bell Laboratories discovered that the
> earth is bathed in a faint glow of radiation
> coming from every direction in the heavens.
> The measurements showed that the
> earth itself could not be the origin of this
> radiation, nor could the radiation come

from the direction of the moon, the sun, or any other particular object in the sky. The entire Universe seemed to be the source.

The two physicists were puzzled by their discovery. They were not thinking about the origin of the Universe, and they did not realize that they had stumbled upon the answer to one of the cosmic mysteries. Scientists who believed in the theory of the Big Bang had long asserted that the Universe must have resembled a white-hot fireball in the very first moments after the Big Bang occurred. Gradually, as the Universe expanded and cooled, the fireball would have become less brilliant, but its radiation would have never disappeared entirely. It was the diffuse glow of this ancient radiation, dating back to the birth of the Universe, that Penzias and Wilson apparently discovered.

...The clincher, which has convinced almost the last doubting Thomas, is that the radiation discovered by Penzias and Wilson has exactly the pattern of wavelengths expected for the light and heat produced in a great explosion.[109]

After reviewing even more evidence for the Big Bang and some of the scientists' reaction to it, which included efforts to get around the clear implications of their work, Jastrow ends with some telling comments:

A sound [scientific] explanation may exist for the explosive birth of our Universe; but if it does, science cannot find out what the explanation is. The scientist's pursuit of the past ends in the moment of creation.

This is an exceedingly strange development, unexpected by all but the theologians. They have always accepted the word of the Bible: In the beginning God created heaven and earth...

...For the scientist who has lived by his faith in the power of reason, the story ends like a bad dream. He has scaled the mountains of ignorance; he is about to conquer the highest peak; as he pulls himself over the final rock, he is greeted by a band of theologians who have been sitting there for centuries.[110]

Science has confirmed that the heavens and the earth came into existence from nothing. Now, if you are an atheist, this poses a problem. Philosopher and atheist Anthony Kenny puts it this way: "According to the big bang theory, the whole matter of the universe began to exist at a particular time in the remote past. A proponent of such a theory, at least if he is an atheist, must believe that the matter of the universe *came from nothing and by nothing.*"[111] For Christians, there's no need to accept such an absurdity that the universe exploded into existence without anything or anyone causing it to happen. We can affirm what the Judeo-Christian faith has always taught: God created the universe *ex nihilo.* Someone (God) caused something (the universe) to come to exist from nothing. That's biblical, reasonable, and now scientifically confirmed.[112]

APPENDIX 2

The Length of Days

All Christians agree that God created the universe. But when it comes to other matters, such as how long he took to create it, Christians disagree. Some of this disagreement revolves around the Hebrew word *yom*, which means "day." This word appears in reference to each of the seven days mentioned in Genesis 1–2. So what does *yom* mean?

Often in Scripture, *yom* refers to a solar day, a twenty-four-hour period (Exodus 20:11), but this isn't the only meaning of the word. In fact, in the Bible, *yom*'s meaning is as elastic as the English word *day*. Along with a solar day, *yom* can refer to:

- the period of natural light (Genesis 1:5)
- metaphorical light (Proverbs 4:18)
- a year or years (Exodus 13:10; 1 Samuel 27:7)
- a particular day (like a calendar day) (Genesis 21:26; Ezra 10:16–17; Haggai 1:1)
- a short or lengthy time period (Genesis 8:22; Deuteronomy 11:21)
- a period of undefined length (Genesis 19:37; Ecclesiastes 7:14; Isaiah 17:11; Obadiah 12–14; Zechariah 4:10)
- a very long time (Psalm 90:4)
- a point of time or moment (Genesis 2:17)
- a period of defeat in battle (Isaiah 9:4; Ezekiel 30:9)

- the past (Genesis 2:4; Numbers 3:13; Deuteronomy 4:10, 32)
- the future (Genesis 2:17; Ruth 4:5)
- important events in salvation history (Numbers 15:23)
- a period of reformation, revelation, temptation, or testing (Genesis 7:4; Exodus 16:35; 24:18; Jonah 3:4)
- a time when salvation is divinely given (Psalm 118:24)
- a time when adoption is divinely achieved (Psalm 2:7)
- predicted events (Isaiah 21:6–7)
- the "Day of the Lord," which can refer to times of judgment or blessing (Isaiah 2; 7:18–25; 10:27; Jeremiah 31:27–40; Amos 5:18; Joel 2:31; Malachi 4:5–6), including all eschatological events

This is not an exhaustive list of the meanings of *yom* in Scripture, but it's enough to demonstrate that the word alone does not indicate it's meaning. It's the context in which the word appears that helps settle what the word means.

So what does *yom* mean in Genesis 1–2? Without trying to come to a definitive answer, the context indicates that *yom* doesn't mean just one thing in every verse it appears. For example, the seventh day is not a solar day. Genesis 2:1–3 reveals that God completed his creation activity; as far as the creation of the heavens and the earth, God's work was finished. Hebrews uses the fact of God's rest after his finished creation work to call on his readers to enter into that rest, which he assumes is still ongoing and accessible to us (Hebrews 4:1–8). So here *yom* refers to all of history since the end of God's creative work and into the everlasting future.

Genesis 2:4 also uses *yom* (translated as "At the time") to refer to all of God's *past* creation work, hence definitely not a solar day.

Then in Genesis 2:17, God uses *yom* in his warning to Adam not to eat from the forbidden tree for "when [in the *yom*] you eat from it you will most certainly die." *Yom* here means "moment" or "point in time." In Genesis 3 when Adam and Eve violate this command, they experience some aspects of death immediately but not physical death for hundreds of years.

So what about the actual days describing creation, the ones apparently sequentially numbered and with the phrase "evening gave way to morning"? Are those solar days? Perhaps, but here are some other considerations.

First, the "days" of Genesis 1 may not be in sequential order despite being numbered one, two, three, and so on. As you learned in Lesson 3, the events of Day 1 correspond to the events of Day 4, those of Day 2 fit well with those of Day 5, and those of Day 3 match up with those of Day 6. Days 1 through 3 indicate the creation of something that needed to be filled, and Days 4 through 6 tell what they were filled with. So the actual sequence of God's creative activity could be the events mentioned in Days 1 and 4, then the events revealed in Days 2 and 5, and then the events detailed in Days 3 and 6. The sequence, then, would not be 1, 2, 3, 4, 5, 6, and 7 but 1/4, 2/5, 3/6, and then 7.

Second, in the Hebrew text, the first five days of Genesis 1 have no definite article ("the") with *yom* or the number used with it. They read "one day," "second day," "third day," "fourth day," and "fifth day"—indefinite uses of *yom*. Day 6 has no definite article with *yom*, but it does with the number, so Bible scholars consider this a definite use of "day," usually translating it "*the* sixth day" (emphasis added). Day 7 appears similarly to Day 6 so is often translated "*the* seventh day" (emphasis added). After reviewing these features of Genesis 1–2 and comparing them to similar passages in the Old Testament, David Sterchi concludes that Genesis "is not implying a chronological sequence of seven days. Instead it is simply presenting a list of seven days. It is not that the list is definitely not chronological. It may be chronological, but the syntax of the list does not require that we read it as such." Moreover, the definiteness of Days 6 and 7 stand out from the other Days. This shows that Days 6 and 7 are unique, with Day 6 the climax of God's creative work, and Day 7 the end of his creative work. So, concludes Sterchi, the seven days of Genesis "are more like a numbered list...Each day was apparently numbered on the basis of its content, not its order in time. This may have allowed the author the freedom to arrange the list of days in an order that better suited his compositional strategy than the actual chronology. It also avoided misrepresenting the true order of events by not using the syntax of chronology." [113] Put another way, the writer of Genesis presented the days in the order of their significance, not the order of their occurrence, putting the most important of the seven days last.

Third, "day" linked with a number does not require that it be a solar day. In Hosea 6:1–2, the prophet calls on his readers "to return to the Lord." Even though Yahweh has "torn us," he will "heal us," and though he has "wounded us," he will "bandage us." Then he adds, "He will revive us after two days," and "He will raise us up on the third day, that we may live before Him" (NASB). Here there's a numbered series of days, but they don't indicate solar days, just indefinite time periods in the future. And then Genesis 2:2–3 has God's creation rest numbered as Day 7, but it clearly includes all of history following the end of God's creation activity.

Fourth, the phrase "evening gave way to morning," if taken strictly, does not indicate 24 hours but perhaps just half a solar day, from sunset to sunrise. It may also be understood figuratively, from darkness to light (indicating enlightenment or revelation) or to indicate "a beginning and end of a definite period of time, just as we refer to 'the dawn of world history' or the 'sunset years of one's life.'"[114] In Job 4:20, "morning and evening" are used in the sense of continually, referring to the brevity and hardship of earthly life.

Fifth, since Genesis 1–2 is describing what God did in terms of time, we would do well to remember that time to God is not what it is to us. The psalmist writes of God, "One thousand years pass before your eyes like yesterday [yom] that quickly faded away, like a night's sleep soon forgotten" (Psalm 90:4).

Finally, outside of Genesis, the creation week reveals to us a pattern we should follow for our work and rest. Exodus 20 says:

> Remember to observe the Sabbath day
> by keeping it holy. You have six days

each week for your ordinary work, but
the seventh day is a Sabbath day of rest
dedicated to the Lord your God...For in six
days the Lord made the heavens, the earth,
the sea, and everything in them; but on the
seventh day he rested. That is why the Lord
blessed the Sabbath day and set it apart as
holy. (vv. 8–9, 11 NLT)

The use of "day" here for the human work week and Sabbath certainly refers to twenty-four-hour days, but that doesn't necessarily mean that the days of God's creation activity are solar days. As Norman Geisler puts it: "It is true that the creation week is compared with a workweek (Ex. 20:11); however, it is not uncommon in the Old Testament to make unit-to-unit comparisons rather than minute-for-minute ones. For example, God appointed forty years of wandering for forty days of disobedience (Num. 14:34). And, in Daniel 9, 490 days equals 490 years (cf. 9:24–27)."[115] Furthermore, the workweek-and-rest pattern refers to years, not days, in Exodus 23:10–11, and then just one verse later goes back to days, indicating the six-one pattern more than tying a specific unit of time to it. And then Deuteronomy 5:12–15, while reiterating the holiness and restfulness of the Sabbath, refers to the Hebrews' many years of Egyptian slavery and God delivering them as the justification for their resting from their labors, not God's rest from his creation activity. In other words, it's the work-rest pattern that matters, not the time unit attached to it.

While more could be said on this matter of the length of days, this is enough to make it clear that the Hebrew word *yom* does not, by itself, settle the matter of whether the Days of Genesis 1–2 are solar days or not.[116]

Endnotes

1 "About The Passion Translation," *The Passion Translation: The New Testament with Psalms, Proverbs, and Song of Songs* (Savage, MN: BroadStreet Publishing Group, 2017), iv.

2 Merrill F. Unger, "Versions of the Scriptures," *The New Unger's Bible Dictionary*, ed. R. K. Harrison (Chicago: Moody Press, 1988), 1342.

3 Allen P. Ross, "Genesis," *The Bible Knowledge Commentary: Old Testament*, ed. John F. Walvoord and Roy B. Zuck (Wheaton, IL: Victor Books, 1985), 15.

4 For more on this, see Norman L. Geisler and William E. Nix, *A General Introduction to the Bible*, revised ed. (Chicago: Moody Press, 1986), 22–24, 240–50. The *Prophets* were the books of Joshua, Judges, (1 and 2) Samuel, (1 and 2) Kings, Isaiah, Jeremiah, Ezekiel, Hosea, Joel, Amos, Obadiah, Jonah, Micah, Nahum, Habakkuk, Zephaniah, Haggai, Zechariah, and Malachi. The *Writings* were Psalms, Job, Proverbs, Ruth, Song of Songs, Ecclesiastes, Lamentations, Esther, Daniel, Ezra-Nehemiah, and (1 and 2) Chronicles.

5 Bruce K. Waltke with Cathi J. Fredricks, *Genesis: A Commentary* (Grand Rapids, MI: Zondervan Academic, 2001), 22.

6 Waltke, *Genesis*, 24.

7 Waltke, *Genesis*, 24.

8 Gleason L. Archer Jr., *A Survey of Old Testament Introduction*, revised ed. (Chicago: Moody Press, 2007), 95–96. Archer's entire discussion of Mosaic authorship is excellent, detailed, and well worth absorbing and pondering (see chapter 8 of his book).

9 Archer, *A Survey of Old Testament Introduction*, 100.

10 There's much more involved in the dating of the Hebrews' time in Egypt, their liberation, and the time they spent in the wilderness of

Sinai than we can mention here. If you would like to explore these matters, see Leon J. Wood, *A Survey of Israel's History*, revised ed. (Grand Rapids, MI: Zondervan, 1986), ch. 5–7; Archer, *A Survey of Old Testament Introduction*, ch. 16; John J. Davis, *Moses and the Gods of Egypt: Studies in the Book of Exodus* (Grand Rapids, MI: Baker Book House, 1971), ch. 1.

11 See Carl Edwin Amerding, "Midian, Midianites," *The New International Dictionary of Biblical Archaeology*, ed. E. M. Blaiklock and R. K. Harrison (Grand Rapids, MI: Zondervan, 1983), 314; and R. L. Alden, "Midian, Midianites," *The Zondervan Pictorial Encyclopedia of the Bible*, ed. Merrill C. Tenney (Grand Rapids, MI: Zondervan, 1976), vol. 4, 220–22.

12 *Theological Wordbook of the Old Testament*, ed. R. Laird Harris (Chicago: Moody Press, 1980), s.v. "toledot," vol. 1, 380.

13 See Allen P. Ross's excellent discussion on the *toledot* formula in his commentary "Genesis," *The Bible Knowledge Commentary*, 22–26.

14 See, for example, P. J. Wiseman, *Clues to Creation in Genesis*, ed. Donald J. Wiseman, revised ed. (London: Marshall, Morgan & Scott, 1977), and R. K. Harrison, *Introduction to the Old Testament* (Grand Rapids, MI: William B. Eerdmans, 1969), 542–65.

15 The NASB translates Genesis 5:1 this way: "This is the book [*seper*] of the generations of Adam."

16 Waltke, *Genesis*, 32.

17 Ross, "Genesis," *The Bible Knowledge Commentary*, 21.

18 Moses Segal, *The Pentateuch: Its Composition and Its Authorship and Other Biblical Studies*, as quoted by Ross, "Genesis," *The Bible Knowledge Commentary*, 21.

19 Ross, "Genesis," *The Bible Knowledge Commentary*, 21.

20 Brian Simmons, "Introduction" to Genesis, TPT, 3–4.

21 You can find many helpful resources in print and online that treat

biblical and church history. Some of the best print resources for biblical history are: Leon J. Wood, *A Survey of Israel's History*, revised ed. (Grand Rapids, MI: Zondervan, 1986); Paul Johnson, *Jesus: A Biography from a Believer* (New York: Viking, 2010); Paul L. Maier, *In the Fullness of Time: A Historian Looks at Christmas, Easter, and the Early Church* (San Francisco: Harper San Francisco, 1991); Richard L. Niswonger, *New Testament History* (Grand Rapids, MI: Zondervan, 1988). Two excellent introductions to the history of Christian thought are: John D. Hannah, *Our Legacy: The History of Christian Doctrine* (Colorado Springs, CO: NavPress, 2001); Kenneth Richard Samples, *Classic Christian Thinkers: An Introduction* (Covina, CA: Reasons to Believe, 2019). Some resources that consider the history of Christianity from the first century to contemporary times are: Paul R. Spickard and Kevin M. Cragg, *God's Peoples: A Social History of Christianity* (Grand Rapids, MI: Baker Books, 1994); A. Kenneth Curtis, J. Stephen Lang, and Randy Peterson, *The 100 Most Important Events in Christian History* (Grand Rapids, MI: Fleming H. Revell, 1991); Paul Johnson, *A History of Christianity* (New York: Atheneum, 1976); Earle E. Cairns, *Christianity through the Centuries: A History of the Christian Church*, 3rd ed. (Grand Rapids, MI: Zondervan, 1996); christianhistoryinstitute.org.

22   Michael Martinez, "How Long Did It Take J. R. R. Tolkien to Write *The Lord of the Rings*?," Middle-Earth.Xenite.org, September 16, 2011, https://middle-earth.xenite.org/how-long-did-it-take-j-r-r-tolkien-to-write-the-lord-of-the-rings.

23   Gordon J. Wenham, *Genesis 1–15, Volume 1*, Word Biblical Commentary series, gen. ed. David A. Hubbard and Glenn W. Barker (Grand Rapids, MI: Zondervan, 1987), 14.

24   Genesis 1:1, note 'c,' TPT.

25   Wenham, *Genesis 1–15*, 15–16.

26   See, for example, Wenham, *Genesis 1–15*, 5–7; Henri Blocher, *In the Beginning: The Opening Chapters of Genesis* (Downers Grove, IL: InterVarsty Press, 1984), 49–56; Waltke, *Genesis*, 56–58.

27 The words in brackets come from Isaiah 45:18, note 'f,' TPT, as an alternate reading.

28 For an excellent explanation of the Trinity, see Norman L. Geisler, *Systematic Theology: Volume Two: God, Creation* (Minneapolis, MN: Bethany House, 2003), ch. 12.

29 On human beings *as* God's image rather than created *in* his image, see Blocher, *In the Beginning*, 84–85, and Genesis 1:26, note 'c,' TPT.

30 Genesis 1:26, note 'c,' TPT.

31 See *"neqeba"* by Milton C. Fisher and *"zakar"* by Thomas E. McComiskey in *Theological Wordbook of the Old Testament*, vol. 1, 596 and vol. 2, 243, respectively; Lawrence O. Richards, "Male and Female," *Expository Dictionary of Bible Words* (Grand Rapids, MI: Zondervan, 1985), 426–28.

32 Wenham, *Genesis 1–15*, 36.

33 Blocher, *In the Beginning*, 57.

34 For more on this and so much more Scripture has to say on the subject of rest and play, see Robert K. Johnston, *The Christian at Play* (Grand Rapids, MI: William B. Eerdmans, 1983).

35 Genesis 2:7, note 'd,' TPT. For more on the Hebrew word for "soul," see Bruce K. Waltke, *"nepesh," Theological Wordbook of the Old Testament*, vol. 2, 587–91.

36 For more on these interpretive options, see Wenham, *Genesis 1–15*, 62–64; Blocher, *In the Beginning*, 122–34; Derek Kidner, *Genesis: An Introduction and Commentary*, Tyndale Old Testament Commentaries, ed. D. J. Wiseman (Downers Grove, IL: InterVarsity Press, 1967), 62–63.

37 Wenham, *Genesis 1–15*, 63.

38 Wenham, *Genesis 1–15*, 63.

39 See Waltke, *Genesis*, 86, and Blocher, *In the Beginning*, 130–33.

40   Genesis 2:23, note 'd,' TPT.

41   Blocher, *In the Beginning*, 98.

42   Wenham walks through the poetic structure of Genesis 2:23, showing the "techniques of Hebrew poetry" used (Wenham, *Genesis 1–15*, 70).

43   Blocher, *In the Beginning*, 96.

44   Carl Schultz, "*'ezer*," *Theological Wordbook of the Old Testament*, vol. 2, 660–61; Walter C. Kaiser Jr., *Hard Sayings of the Old Testament* (Downers Grove, IL: InterVarsity Press, 1988), ch. 3.

45   Genesis 2:18, note 'g,' TPT.

46   Earl S. Kalland, "*dabaq*," *Theological Wordbook of the Old Testament*, vol. 1, 177–78.

47   Blocher, *In the Beginning*, 109.

48   For more on this prophecy, see *TPT: The Book of Isaiah: 12-Lesson Study Guide*, gen. ed. Dr. Brian Simmons (Savage, MN: BroadStreet Publishing Group, 2020), 63–65; John A. Martin, "Isaiah," *The Bible Knowledge Commentary: Old Testament*, 1059–62.

49   C. Fred Dickason, *Angels: Elect and Evil* (Chicago: Moody Press, 1975), 128.

50   Charles H. Dyer, "Ezekiel," *The Bible Knowledge Commentary: Old Testament*, 1283.

51   Blocher, *In the Beginning*, 171–72.

52   For more on death in Scripture, see Lothar Coenen, "Death, Kill, Sleep," *The New International Dictionary of New Testament Theology*, ed. Colin Brown, 3 vols. (Grand Rapids, MI: Zondervan, 1975), vol. 1, 429–47.

53   Blocher, *In the Beginning*, 179.

54   Genesis 3:21, note 'c,' TPT.

55   Waltke, *Genesis*, 97.

56   Genesis 4:5, note 'h,' TPT.

57   Wenham, *Genesis 1–15*, 106.

58   Waltke, *Genesis*, 98.

59   Gleason L. Archer, *Encyclopedia of Bible Difficulties* (Grand Rapids, MI: Zondervan, 1982), 77.

60   Genesis 9:6 affirms that, even after humanity's initial sin, we still bear the image of God, which is good. Also, Paul states that "everything that God created *is* good" (1 Timothy 4:4 NIV, emphasis added), not *was* good. Human beings and the rest of God's creation are still good in their being—in what they are—but sin has damaged his creation. As Geisler explains, "Sin *effaces* but does not *erase* the image of God in human beings; it is *marred* but not *eliminated*. Even the most vile of human beings retain God's likeness, be it oh so vitiated within" (Norman L. Geisler, *Systematic Theology: Volume Three: Sin, Salvation* [Minneapolis, MN: Bethany House, 2004], 146).

61   Wenham, *Genesis 1–15*, 139.

62   This interpretation is defended by Gleason Archer in his *Encyclopedia of Bible Difficulties*, 79–80.

63   Genesis 6:2, note 'c,' TPT.

64   Waltke, *Genesis*, 116.

65   Waltke, *Genesis*, 116. Waltke is describing Meredith Kline's interpretation. Kline presents this in his essay "Divine Kingship and Sons of God in Genesis 6:1–4," *Westminster Theological Journal* (1962), vol. 24, 187–204.

66   Genesis 6:2, note 'c,' TPT.

67   Archer, *Encyclopedia of Bible Difficulties*, 80.

68   Norman Geisler and Thomas Howe, *When Critics Ask: A Popular*

Handbook on Bible Difficulties (Wheaton, IL: Victor Books, 1992), 40–41. See also Waltke, *Genesis*, 117: "The best interpretation is to combine the 'angelic' interpretation with the 'divine king' view. The tyrants were demon possessed." For more on "the mighty ones of old, warriors of renown" (Genesis 6:4), see study note 'e' for that passage in TPT.

69 Elvin Hatch, "Culture," *The Social Encyclopedia*, ed. Adam Kuper and Jessica Kuper, revised ed. (New York: Routledge, 1989), 178.

70 Geisler and Howe, *When Critics Ask*, 42.

71 Archer, *A Survey of Old Testament Introduction*, 176.

72 Genesis 7:11, note 'e,' TPT.

73 Some Bible scholars have argued that the flood event was local or regional, not worldwide. One of these is Bernard Ramm in his book *The Christian View of Science and Scripture* (Grand Rapids, MI: William B. Eerdmans, 1954), 156–69. Gleason Archer responds to Ramm's arguments in his *A Survey of Old Testament Introduction*, 171–80. Archer also supplies a number of other reasons for viewing the flood as worldwide rather than regional. A more extensive case for a global flood is found in *The Genesis Flood* by John C. Whitcomb and Henry M. Morris (Nutley, NJ: Presbyterian and Reformed, 1961).

74 Waltke, *Genesis*, 148, 147.

75 Waltke, *Genesis*, 149.

76 Waltke, *Genesis*, 150.

77 Waltke, *Genesis*, 151.

78 Waltke, *Genesis*, 153.

79 Ross, "Genesis," *The Bible Knowledge Commentary*, 41–42.

80 Wenham, *Genesis 1–15*, 208.

81 Waltke, *Genesis*, 161.

82 Saint Augustine, *The City of God*, trans. Marcus Dods, The Modern Library series (New York: Random House, 1950), 12.9. Dave Unander, in his book *Shattering the Myth of Race: Genetic Realities and Biblical Truths* (Valley Forge, PA: Judson Press, 2000), explains the scientific support for the one-human-race view and how it fits with historic Christian teaching.

83 Allen P. Ross, "The Table of Nations in Genesis 10—Its Structure," *Bibliotheca Sacra* (October–December 1980), 347.

84 Ross, "The Table of Nations in Genesis 10—Its Structure," 346.

85 Ross, "The Table of Nations in Genesis 10—Its Structure," 342–43.

86 Ross, "The Table of Nations in Genesis 10—Its Structure," 344.

87 Wenham, *Genesis 1–15*, 214.

88 Wenham, *Genesis 1–15*, 228; Kidner, *Genesis*, 108.

89 Waltke, *Genesis*, 172.

90 Wenham, *Genesis 1–15*, 230.

91 Waltke, *Genesis*, 173.

92 Ross, "Genesis," *The Bible Knowledge Commentary*, 44.

93 Unger, *The New Unger's Bible Dictionary*, s.v. "Shinar," 1185–86.

94 The issues around human language and how we use it to talk about God are many and complex. To explore them, you will find excellent help in these resources by Christian theologian and philosopher Norman L. Geisler: "Analogy, Principle of," *Baker Encyclopedia of Christian Apologetics* (Grand Rapids, MI: Baker Books, 1999), 17–22; *Systematic Theology: Volume One: Introduction, Bible* (Minneapolis, MN: Bethany House, 2003), ch. 9.

95 The Bible is full of various kinds of analogical speech, including the anthropomorphic language used in Genesis 11:5. A classic treatment of these uses of speech as they appear in Scripture is *Figures of*

Speech Used in the Bible, by E. W. Bullinger, reprint ed. (Grand Rapids, MI: Baker Book House, 1968).

96 Blocher, *In the Beginning*, 206–207.

97 TPT, note 'b' for John 1:1.

98 Wenham, *Genesis 1–15*, 245.

99 For statements of these philosophical arguments against an eternal universe, see J. P. Moreland, *Scaling the Secular City: A Defense of Christianity* (Grand Rapids, MI: Baker Book House, 1987), ch. 1; William Lane Craig, *The Existence of God and the Beginning of the Universe* (San Bernardino, CA: Here's Life Publishers, 1979), ch. 2; Geisler, "*Kalam* Cosmological Argument," *Baker Encyclopedia of Christian Apologetics*, 399–401.

100 Robert Jastrow, *God and the Astronomers* (New York: W. W. Norton & Co., 1978), 14.

101 J. Richard Gott III, James E. Gunn, David N. Schramm, and Beatrice M. Tinsley, "Will the Universe Expand Forever?" *Scientific American* (March 1976), 65.

102 Jastrow, *God and the Astronomers*, 11.

103 Jastrow, *God and the Astronomers*, 23.

104 Jastrow, *God and the Astronomers*, 28–29.

105 Hugh Ross, "Astronomical Evidences for a Personal, Transcendent God," *The Creation Hypothesis: Scientific Evidence for an Intelligent Designer*, ed. J. P. Moreland (Downers Grove, IL: InterVarsity Press, 1994), 145.

106 Jastrow, *God and the Astronomers*, 43.

107 Jastrow, *God and the Astronomers*, 47.

108 As stated by Geisler, "Thermodynamics, Laws of," *Baker Encyclopedia of Christian Apologetics*, 724. For a more detailed discussion of

this second law, see Gordon W. F. Drake, "Thermodynamics," in *Britannica*, accessed March 21, 2021, https://www.britannica.com/science/thermodynamics.

109 Jastrow, *God and the Astronomers*, 14–15.

110 Jastrow, *God and the Astronomers*, 115, 116.

111 Anthony Kenny, *The Five Ways: Thomas Aquinas' Proofs of God's Existence* (New York: Schocken Books, 1969), 66.

112 Some scientists have attempted to deny what the Big Bang requires—a Beginner, a cause that brought time, space, and matter into existence. For explanations and criticisms of these theoretical attempts, see Geisler, "Big Bang Theory," *Baker Encyclopedia of Christian Apologetics*, 102–106; Lee Strobel, *The Case for a Creator: A Journalist Investigates Scientific Evidence That Points toward God* (Grand Rapids, MI: Zondervan, 2004), ch. 5, "The Evidence of Cosmology: Beginning with a Bang," an interview with William Lane Craig; Robert J. Spitzer, *New Proofs for the Existence of God: Contributions of Contemporary Physics and Philosophy* (Grand Rapids, MI: William B. Eerdmans, 2010).

113 David A. Sterchi, "Does Genesis 1 Provide a Chronological Sequence?" *Journal of the Evangelical Theological Society* (December 1996), vol. 1, no. 4, 533–34, 536.

114 Geisler, "Genesis, Days of," *Baker Encyclopedia of Christian Apologetics*, 271.

115 Geisler, *Systematic Theology*, vol. 2, 640.

116 For more on *yom* and its meaning in the Old Testament, see Geisler, "Genesis, Days of," *Baker Encyclopedia of Christian Apologetics*, 270–73; Richards, "Day," *Expository Dictionary of Bible Words*, 210–11; W. E. Vine, "Day," *An Expository Dictionary of Biblical Words*, ed. Merrill F. Unger and William White (Nashville, TN: Thomas Nelson, 1985), 54–55; Leonard J. Coppes, "*yom*," *Theological Wordbook of the Old Testament*, vol. 1, 370–71; S. Barabas, "Day," *The Zondervan Pictorial Encyclopedia of the Bible*, vol. 2, 45–46.